ARE PRISONS OBSOLETE?

Angela Y. Davis

An Open Media Book

SEVEN STORIES PRESS
New York

In Canada: Hushion House, 36 Northline Road, Toronto, Ontario M4B 3E2

In the U.K.: Turnaround Publisher Services Ltd., Unit 3, Olympia Trading Estate, Coburg Road, Wood Green, London N22 6TZ

In Australia: Palgrave Macmillan, 627 Chapel Street, South Yarra, VIC 3141

Cover design and photos: Greg Ruggiero

ISBN 1-58322-581-1

Printed in Canada.

9 8 7 6 5 4 3 2 1

Contents

Acknowledgments

I should not be listed as the sole author of this book, for its ideas reflect various forms of collaboration over the last six years with activists, scholars, prisoners, and cultural workers who have tried to reveal and contest the impact of the prison industrial complex on the lives of people—within and outside prisons—throughout the world. The organizing committee for the 1998 Berkeley conference, Critical Resistance: Beyond the Prison Industrial Complex, included Bo (rita d. brown), Ellen Barry, Jennifer Beach, Rose Braz, Julie Browne, Cynthia Chandler, Kamari Clarke, Leslie DiBenedetto Skopek, Gita Drury, Rayne Galbraith, Ruthie Gilmore, Naneen Karraker, Terry Kupers, Rachel Lederman, Joyce Miller, Dorsey Nunn, Dylan Rodriguez, Eli Rosenblatt, Jane Segal, Cassandra Shaylor, Andrea Smith, Nancy Stoller, Julia Sudbury, Robin Templeton, and Suran Thrift. In the long process of coordinating plans for this conference, which attracted over three thousand people, we worked through a number of the questions that I raise in this book. I thank the members of that committee, including those who used the conference as a foundation to build the organization Critical Resistance. In 2000, I was a member of a University of California Humanities Research Institute Resident Research Group and had the opportunity to partic-

ipate in regular discussions on many of these issues. I thank the members of the group—Gina Dent, Ruth Gilmore, Avery Gordon, David Goldberg, Nancy Schepper Hughes, and Sandy Barringer—for their invaluable insights. Cassandra Shaylor and I coauthored a report to the 2001 World Conference Against Racism on women of color and the prison industrial complex—a number of whose ideas have made their way into this book. I have also drawn from a number of other recent articles I have published in various collections. Over the last five years Gina Dent and I have made numerous presentations together, published together, and engaged in protracted conversations on what it means to do scholarly and activist work that can encourage us all to imagine a world without prisons. I thank her for reading the manuscript and I am deeply appreciative of her intellectual and emotional support. Finally, I thank Greg Ruggiero, the editor of this series, for his patience and encouragement.

1

Introduction–Prison Reform or Prison Abolition?

In most parts of the world, it is taken for granted that whoever is convicted of a serious crime will be sent to prison. In some countries—including the United States—where capital punishment has not yet been abolished, a small but significant number of people are sentenced to death for what are considered especially grave crimes. Many people are familiar with the campaign to abolish the death penalty. In fact, it has already been abolished in most countries. Even the staunchest advocates of capital punishment acknowledge the fact that the death penalty faces serious challenges. Few people find life without the death penalty difficult to imagine.

On the other hand, the prison is considered an inevitable and permanent feature of our social lives. Most people are quite surprised to hear that the prison abolition movement also has a long history—one that dates back to the historical appearance of the prison as the main form of punishment. In fact, the most natural reaction is to assume that prison activists—even those who consciously refer to themselves as "antiprison activists"—are simply trying to ameliorate prison conditions or perhaps to reform the prison in more fundamental ways. In most circles prison abolition is simply unthinkable and implausible. Prison abolitionists are dis-

9

missed as utopians and idealists whose ideas are at best unrealistic and impracticable, and, at worst, mystifying and foolish. This is a measure of how difficult it is to envision a social order that does not rely on the threat of sequestering people in dreadful places designed to separate them from their communities and families. The prison is considered so "natural" that it is extremely hard to imagine life without it.

It is my hope that this book will encourage readers to question their own assumptions about the prison. Many people have already reached the conclusion that the death penalty is an outmoded form of punishment that violates basic principles of human rights. It is time, I believe, to encourage similar conversations about the prison. During my own career as an antiprison activist I have seen the population of U.S. prisons increase with such rapidity that many people in black, Latino, and Native American communities now have a far greater chance of going to prison than of getting a decent education. When many young people decide to join the military service in order to avoid the inevitability of a stint in prison, it should cause us to wonder whether we should not try to introduce better alternatives.

The question of whether the prison has become an obsolete institution has become especially urgent in light of the fact that more than two million people (out of a world total of nine million) now inhabit U.S. prisons, jails, youth facilities, and immigrant detention centers. Are we willing to relegate ever larger numbers of people from racially oppressed communities to an isolated existence marked by authoritarian regimes, violence, disease, and technologies of seclusion that produce severe mental instability? According to a recent study, there may be twice as many people suffering from mental illness who are in jails and prisons than there are in all psychiatric hospitals in the United States combined.

60's: 200,000
Today: 2 million !

When I first became involved in antiprison activism during the late 1960s, I was astounded to learn that there were then close to two hundred thousand people in prison. Had anyone told me that in three decades ten times as many people would be locked away in cages, I would have been absolutely incredulous. I imagine that I would have responded something like this: "As racist and undemocratic as this country may be [remember, during that period, the demands of the Civil Rights movement had not yet been consolidated], I do not believe that the U.S. government will be able to lock up so many people without producing powerful public resistance. No, this will never happen, not unless this country plunges into fascism." That might have been my reaction thirty years ago. The reality is that we were called upon to inaugurate the twenty-first century by accepting the fact that two million people—a group larger than the population of many countries—are living their lives in places like Sing Sing, Leavenworth, San Quentin, and Alderson Federal Reformatory for Women. The gravity of these numbers becomes even more apparent when we consider that the U.S. population in general is less than five percent of the world's total, whereas more than twenty percent of the world's combined prison population can be claimed by the United States. In Elliott Currie's words, "[t]he prison has become a looming presence in our society to an extent unparalleled in our history or that of any other industrial democracy. Short of major wars, mass incarceration has been the most thoroughly implemented government social program of our time."[2]

In thinking about the possible obsolescence of the prison, we should ask how it is that so many people could end up in prison without major debates regarding the efficacy of incarceration. When the drive to produce more prisons and incar-

5% —
of
20% +

cerate ever larger numbers of people occurred in the 1980s during what is known as the Reagan era, politicians argued that "tough on crime" stances—including certain imprisonment and longer sentences—would keep communities free of crime. However, the practice of mass incarceration during that period had little or no effect on official crime rates. In fact, the most obvious pattern was that larger prison populations led not to safer communities, but, rather, to even larger prison populations. Each new prison spawned yet another new prison. And as the U.S. prison system expanded, so did corporate involvement in construction, provision of goods and services, and use of prison labor. Because of the extent to which prison building and operation began to attract vast amounts of capital—from the construction industry to food and health care provision—in a way that recalled the emergence of the military industrial complex, we began to refer to a "prison industrial complex."[3]

Consider the case of California, whose landscape has been thoroughly prisonized over the last twenty years. The first state prison in California was San Quentin, which opened in 1852.[4] Folsom, another well-known institution, opened in 1880. Between 1880 and 1933, when a facility for women was opened in Tehachapi, there was not a single new prison constructed. In 1952, the California Institution for Women opened and Tehachapi became a new prison for men. In all, between 1852 and 1955, nine prisons were constructed in California. Between 1962 and 1965, two camps were established, along with the California Rehabilitation Center. Not a single prison opened during the second half of the sixties, nor during the entire decade of the 1970s.

However, a massive project of prison construction was initiated during the 1980s—that is, during the years of the Reagan presidency. Nine prisons, including the Northern California

Facility for Women, were opened between 1984 and 1989. Recall that it had taken more than a hundred years to build the first nine California prisons. In less than a single decade, the number of California prisons doubled. And during the 1990s, twelve new prisons were opened, including two more for women. In 1995 the Valley State Prison for Women was opened. According to its mission statement, it "provides 1,980 women's beds for California's overcrowded prison system." However, in 2002, there were 3,570 prisoners[5] and the other two women's prisons were equally overcrowded.

There are now thirty-three prisons, thirty-eight camps, sixteen community correctional facilities, and five tiny prisoner mother facilities in California. In 2002 there were 157,979 people incarcerated in these institutions, including approximately twenty thousand people whom the state holds for immigration violations. The racial composition of this prison population is revealing. Latinos, who are now in the majority, account for 35.2 percent; African-Americans 30 percent, and white prisoners 29.2 percent.[6] There are now more women in prison in the state of California than there were in the entire country in the early 1970s. In fact, California can claim the largest women's prison in the world, Valley State Prison for Women, with its more than thirty-five hundred inhabitants. Located in the same town as Valley State and literally across the street is the second-largest women's prison in the world—Central California Women's Facility—whose population in 2002 also hovered around thirty-five hundred.[7]

If you look at a map of California depicting the location of the thirty-three state prisons, you will see that the only area that is not heavily populated by prisons is the area north of Sacramento. Still, there are two prisons in the town of Susanville, and Pelican Bay, one of the state's notorious super-maximum security prisons, is near the Oregon border.

California artist Sandow Birk was inspired by the colonizing of the landscape by prisons to produce a series of thirty-three landscape paintings of these institutions and their surroundings. They are collected in his book *Incarcerated: Visions of California in the Twenty-first Century.*[8]

I present this brief narrative of the prisonization of the California landscape in order to allow readers to grasp how easy it was to produce a massive system of incarceration with the implicit consent of the public. Why were people so quick to assume that locking away an increasingly large proportion of the U.S. population would help those who live in the free world feel safer and more secure? This question can be formulated in more general terms. Why do prisons tend to make people think that their own rights and liberties are more secure than they would be if prisons did not exist? What other reasons might there have been for the rapidity with which prisons began to colonize the California landscape?

Geographer Ruth Gilmore describes the expansion of prisons in California as "a geographical solution to socio-economic problems."[9] Her analysis of the prison industrial complex in California describes these developments as a response to surpluses of capital, land, labor, and state capacity.

> California's new prisons are sited on devalued rural land, most, in fact on formerly irrigated agricultural acres . . . The State bought land sold by big landowners. And the State assured the small, depressed towns now shadowed by prisons that the new, recession-proof, non-polluting industry would jump-start local redevelopment.[10]

But, as Gilmore points out, neither the jobs nor the more general economic revitalization promised by prisons has

occurred. At the same time, this promise of progress helps us to understand why the legislature and California's voters decided to approve the construction of all these new prisons. People wanted to believe that prisons would not only reduce crime, they would also provide jobs and stimulate economic development in out-of-the-way places.

At bottom, there is one fundamental question: Why do we take prison for granted? While a relatively small proportion of the population has ever directly experienced life inside prison, this is not true in poor black and Latino communities. Neither is it true for Native Americans or for certain Asian-American communities. But even among those people who must regrettably accept prison sentences—especially young people—as an ordinary dimension of community life, it is hardly acceptable to engage in serious public discussions about prison life or radical alternatives to prison. It is as if prison were an inevitable fact of life, like birth and death.

On the whole, people tend to take prisons for granted. It is difficult to imagine life without them. At the same time, there is reluctance to face the realities hidden within them, a fear of thinking about what happens inside them. Thus, the prison is present in our lives and, at the same time, it is absent from our lives. To think about this simultaneous presence and absence is to begin to acknowledge the part played by ideology in shaping the way we interact with our social surroundings. We take prisons for granted but are often afraid to face the realities they produce. After all, no one wants to go to prison. Because it would be too agonizing to cope with the possibility that anyone, including ourselves, could become a prisoner, we tend to think of the prison as disconnected from our own lives. This is even true for some of us, women as well as men, who have already experienced imprisonment.

We thus think about imprisonment as a fate reserved for others, a fate reserved for the "evildoers," to use a term recently popularized by George W. Bush. Because of the persistent power of racism, "criminals" and "evildoers" are, in the collective imagination, fantasized as people of color. The prison therefore functions ideologically as an abstract site into which undesirables are deposited, relieving us of the responsibility of thinking about the real issues afflicting those communities from which prisoners are drawn in such disproportionate numbers. This is the ideological work that the prison performs—it relieves us of the responsibility of seriously engaging with the problems of our society, especially those produced by racism and, increasingly, global capitalism.

What, for example, do we miss if we try to think about prison expansion without addressing larger economic developments? We live in an era of migrating corporations. In order to escape organized labor in this country—and thus higher wages, benefits, and so on—corporations roam the world in search of nations providing cheap labor pools. This corporate migration thus leaves entire communities in shambles. Huge numbers of people lose jobs and prospects for future jobs. Because the economic base of these communities is destroyed, education and other surviving social services are profoundly affected. This process turns the men, women, and children who live in these damaged communities into perfect candidates for prison.

In the meantime, corporations associated with the punishment industry reap profits from the system that manages prisoners and acquire a clear stake in the continued growth of prison populations. Put simply, this is the era of the prison industrial complex. The prison has become a black hole into which the detritus of contemporary capitalism is deposited. Mass imprisonment generates profits as it devours social

wealth, and thus it tends to reproduce the very conditions that lead people to prison. There are thus real and often quite complicated connections between the deindustrialization of the economy—a process that reached its peak during the 1980s—and the rise of mass imprisonment, which also began to spiral during the Reagan-Bush era. However, the demand for more prisons was represented to the public in simplistic terms. More prisons were needed because there was more crime. Yet many scholars have demonstrated that by the time the prison-construction boom began, official crime statistics were already falling. Moreover, draconian drug laws were being enacted, and "three-strikes" provisions were on the agendas of many states.

In order to understand the proliferation of prisons and the rise of the prison industrial complex, it might be helpful to think further about the reasons we so easily take prisons for granted. In California, as we have seen, almost two-thirds of existing prisons were opened during the eighties and nineties. Why was there no great outcry? Why was there such an obvious level of comfort with the prospect of many new prisons? A partial answer to this question has to do with the way we consume media images of the prison, even as the realities of imprisonment are hidden from almost all who have not had the misfortune of doing time. Cultural critic Gina Dent has pointed out that our sense of familiarity with the prison comes in part from representations of prisons in film and other visual media.

> The history of visuality linked to the prison is also a main reinforcement of the institution of the prison as a naturalized part of our social landscape. The history of film has always been wedded to the representation of incarceration. Thomas Edison's

first films (dating back to the 1901 reenactment presented as newsreel, *Execution of Czolgosz with Panorama of Auburn Prison*) included footage of the darkest recesses of the prison. Thus, the prison is wedded to our experience of visuality, creating also a sense of its permanence as an institution. We also have a constant flow of Hollywood prison films, in fact a genre.[11]

Some of the most well known prison films are: *I Want to Live*, *Papillon*, *Cool Hand Luke*, and *Escape from Alcatraz*. It also bears mentioning that television programming has become increasingly saturated with images of prisons. Some recent documentaries include the A&E series *The Big House*, which consists of programs on San Quentin, Alcatraz, Leavenworth, and Alderson Federal Reformatory for Women. The long-running HBO program *Oz* has managed to persuade many viewers that they know exactly what goes on in male maximum-security prisons.

But even those who do not consciously decide to watch a documentary or dramatic program on the topic of prisons inevitably consume prison images, whether they choose to or not, by the simple fact of watching movies or TV. It is virtually impossible to avoid consuming images of prison. In 1997, I was myself quite astonished to find, when I interviewed women in three Cuban prisons, that most of them narrated their prior awareness of prisons—that is, before they were actually incarcerated—as coming from the many Hollywood films they had seen. The prison is one of the most important features of our image environment. This has caused us to take the existence of prisons for granted. The prison has become a key ingredient of our common sense. It is there, all around us. We do not question whether it should

exist. It has become so much a part of our lives that it requires a great feat of the imagination to envision life beyond the prison.

This is not to dismiss the profound changes that have occurred in the way public conversations about the prison are conducted. Ten years ago, even as the drive to expand the prison system reached its zenith, there were very few critiques of this process available to the public. In fact, most people had no idea about the immensity of this expansion. This was the period during which internal changes—in part through the application of new technologies—led the U.S. prison system in a much more repressive direction. Whereas previous classifications had been confined to low, medium, and maximum security, a new category was invented—that of the super-maximum security prison, or the supermax. The turn toward increased repression in a prison system, distinguished from the beginning of its history by its repressive regimes, caused some journalists, public intellectuals, and progressive agencies to oppose the growing reliance on prisons to solve social problems that are actually exacerbated by mass incarceration.

In 1990, the Washington-based Sentencing Project published a study of U.S. populations in prison and jail, and on parole and probation, which concluded that one in four black men between the ages of twenty and twenty-nine were among these numbers.[1] Five years later, a second study revealed that this percentage had soared to almost one in three (32.2 percent). Moreover, more than one in ten Latino men in this same age range were in jail or prison, or on probation or parole. The second study also revealed that the group experiencing the greatest increase was black women, whose imprisonment increased by seventy-eight percent.[3] According to the Bureau of Justice Statistics, African-

Americans as a whole now represent the majority of state and federal prisoners, with a total of 803,400 black inmates—118,600 more than the total number of white inmates.[14] During the late 1990s major articles on prison expansion appeared in *Newsweek, Harper's, Emerge,* and *Atlantic Monthly.* Even Colin Powell raised the question of the rising number of black men in prison when he spoke at the 2000 Republican National Convention, which declared George W. Bush its presidential candidate.

Over the last few years the previous absence of critical positions on prison expansion in the political arena has given way to proposals for prison reform. While public discourse has become more flexible, the emphasis is almost inevitably on generating the changes that will produce a *better* prison system. In other words, the increased flexibility that has allowed for critical discussion of the problems associated with the expansion of prisons also restricts this discussion to the question of prison reform.

As important as some reforms may be—the elimination of sexual abuse and medical neglect in women's prison, for example—frameworks that rely exclusively on reforms help to produce the stultifying idea that nothing lies beyond the prison. Debates about strategies of decarceration, which should be the focal point of our conversations on the prison crisis, tend to be marginalized when reform takes the center stage. The most immediate question today is how to prevent the further expansion of prison populations and how to bring as many imprisoned women and men as possible back into what prisoners call "the free world." How can we move to decriminalize drug use and the trade in sexual services? How can we take seriously strategies of restorative rather than exclusively punitive justice? Effective alternatives involve both transformation of the techniques for addressing

"crime" and of the social and economic conditions that track so many children from poor communities, and especially communities of color, into the juvenile system and then on to prison. The most difficult and urgent challenge today is that of creatively exploring new terrains of justice, where the prison no longer serves as our major anchor.

2

Slavery, Civil Rights, and Abolitionist Perspectives Toward Prison

"Advocates of incarceration . . . hoped that the penitentiary would *rehabilitate* its inmates. Whereas philoso-
phers perceived a ceaseless state of war between chattel
slaves and their masters, criminologists hoped to negoti-
ate a peace treaty of sorts within the prison walls. Yet
herein lurked a paradox: if the penitentiary's internal
regime resembled that of the plantation so closely that the
two were often loosely equated, how could the prison pos-
sibly function to rehabilitate criminals?"

—Adam Jay Hirsch[15]

The prison is not the only institution that has posed complex
challenges to the people who have lived with it and have
become so inured to its presence that they could not con-
ceive of society without it. Within the history of the United
States the system of slavery immediately comes to mind.
Although as early as the American Revolution antislavery
advocates promoted the elimination of African bondage, it
took almost a century to achieve the abolition of the "peculiar institution." White antislavery abolitionists such as John
Brown and William Lloyd Garrison were represented in the

dominant media of the period as extremists and fanatics. When Frederick Douglass embarked on his career as an anti-slavery orator, white people—even those who were passionate abolitionists—refused to believe that a black slave could display such intelligence. The belief in the permanence of slavery was so widespread that even white abolitionists found it difficult to imagine black people as equals.

It took a long and violent civil war in order to legally dis-establish the "peculiar institution." Even though the Thirteenth Amendment to the U.S. Constitution outlawed involuntary servitude, white supremacy continued to be embraced by vast numbers of people and became deeply inscribed in new institutions. One of these post-slavery institutions was lynching, which was widely accepted for many decades thereafter. Thanks to the work of figures such as Ida B. Wells, an antilynching campaign was gradually legitimized during the first half of the twentieth century. The NAACP, an organization that continues to conduct legal challenges against discrimination, evolved from these efforts to abolish lynching.

Segregation ruled the South until it was outlawed a century after the abolition of slavery. Many people who lived under Jim Crow could not envision a legal system defined by racial equality. When the governor of Alabama personally attempted to prevent Arthurine Lucy from enrolling in the University of Alabama, his stance represented the inability to imagine black and white people ever peaceably living and studying together. "Segregation today, segregation tomorrow, segregation forever" are the most well known words of this politician, who was forced to repudiate them some years later when segregation had proved far more vulnerable than he could have imagined.

Although government, corporations, and the dominant

media try to represent racism as an unfortunate aberration of the past that has been relegated to the graveyard of U.S. history, it continues to profoundly influence contemporary structures, attitudes, and behaviors. Nevertheless, anyone who would dare to call for the reintroduction of slavery, the organization of lynch mobs, or the reestablishment of legal segregation would be summarily dismissed. But it should be remembered that the ancestors of many of today's most ardent liberals could not have imagined life without slavery, life without lynching, or life without segregation. The 2001 World Conference Against Racism, Racial Discrimination, Xenophobia, and Related Intolerances held in Durban, South Africa, divulged the immensity of the global task of eliminating racism. There may be many disagreements regarding what counts as racism and what are the most effective strategies to eliminate it. However, especially with the downfall of the apartheid regime in South Africa, there is a global consensus that racism should not define the future of the planet.

I have referred to these historical examples of efforts to dismantle racist institutions because they have considerable relevance to our discussion of prisons and prison abolition. It is true that slavery, lynching, and segregation acquired such a stalwart ideological quality that many, if not most, could not foresee their decline and collapse. Slavery, lynching, and segregation are certainly compelling examples of social institutions that, like the prison, were once considered to be as everlasting as the sun. Yet, in the case of all three examples, we can point to movements that assumed the radical stance of announcing the obsolescence of these institutions. It may help us gain perspective on the prison if we try to imagine how strange and discomforting the debates about the obsolescence of slavery must have been to those who took the "peculiar institution" for granted—and especially to those

who reaped direct benefits from this dreadful system of racist exploitation. And even though there was widespread resistance among black slaves, there were even some among them who assumed that they and their progeny would be always subjected to the tyranny of slavery.

I have introduced three abolition campaigns that were eventually more or less successful to make the point that social circumstances transform and popular attitudes shift, in part in response to organized social movements. But I have also evoked these historical campaigns because they all targeted some expression of racism. U.S. chattel slavery was a system of forced labor that relied on racist ideas and beliefs to justify the relegation of people of African descent to the legal status of property. Lynching was an extralegal institution that surrendered thousands of African-American lives to the violence of ruthless racist mobs. Under segregation, black people were legally declared second-class citizens, for whom voting, job, education, and housing rights were drastically curtailed, if they were available at all.

What is the relationship between these historical expressions of racism and the role of the prison system today? Exploring such connections may offer us a different perspective on the current state of the punishment industry. If we are already persuaded that racism should not be allowed to define the planet's future and if we can successfully argue that prisons are racist institutions, this may lead us to take seriously the prospect of declaring prisons obsolete.

For the moment I am concentrating on the history of antiblack racism in order to make the point that the prison reveals congealed forms of antiblack racism that operate in clandestine ways. In other words, they are rarely recognized as racist. But there are other racialized histories that have affected the development of the U.S. punishment system as

well—the histories of Latinos, Native Americans, and Asian-Americans. These racisms also congeal and combine in the prison. Because we are so accustomed to talking about race in terms of black and white, we often fail to recognize and contest expressions of racism that target people of color who are not black. Consider the mass arrests and detention of people of Middle Eastern, South Asian, or Muslim heritage in the aftermath of the September 11, 2001 attacks on the Pentagon and World Trade Center.

This leads us to two important questions: Are prisons racist institutions? Is racism so deeply entrenched in the institution of the prison that it is not possible to eliminate one without eliminating the other? These are questions that we should keep in mind as we examine the historical links between U.S. slavery and the early penitentiary system. The penitentiary as an institution that simultaneously punished and rehabilitated its inhabitants was a new system of punishment that first made its appearance in the United States around the time of the American Revolution. This new system was based on the replacement of capital and corporal punishment by incarceration.

Imprisonment itself was new neither to the United States nor to the world, but until the creation of this new institution called the penitentiary, it served as a prelude to punishment. People who were to be subjected to some form of corporal punishment were detained in prison until the execution of the punishment. With the penitentiary, incarceration became the punishment itself. As is indicated in the designation "penitentiary," imprisonment was regarded as rehabilitative and the penitentiary prison was devised to provide convicts with the conditions for reflecting on their crimes and, through penitence, for reshaping their habits and even their souls. Although some antislavery advocates spoke out

against this new system of punishment during the revolutionary period, the penitentiary was generally viewed as a progressive reform, linked to the larger campaign for the rights of citizens.

In many ways, the penitentiary *was* a vast improvement over the many forms of capital and corporal punishment inherited from the English. However, the contention that prisoners would refashion themselves if only given the opportunity to reflect and labor in solitude and silence disregarded the impact of authoritarian regimes of living and work. Indeed, there were significant similarities between slavery and the penitentiary prison. Historian Adam Jay Hirsch has pointed out:

> One may perceive in the penitentiary many reflections of chattel slavery as it was practiced in the South. Both institutions subordinated their subjects to the will of others. Like Southern slaves, prison inmates followed a daily routine specified by their superiors. Both institutions reduced their subjects to dependence on others for the supply of basic human services such as food and shelter. Both isolated their subjects from the general population by confining them to a fixed habitat. And both frequently coerced their subjects to work, often for longer hours and for less compensation than free laborers.[16]

As Hirsch has observed, both institutions deployed similar forms of punishment, and prison regulations were, in fact, very similar to the Slave Codes—the laws that deprived enslaved human beings of virtually all rights. Moreover, both prisoners and slaves were considered to have pronounced proclivities to crime. People sentenced to the penitentiary in

the North, white and black alike, were popularly represented as having a strong kinship to enslaved black people.[17]

The ideologies governing slavery and those governing punishment were profoundly linked during the earliest period of U.S. history. While free people could be legally sentenced to punishment by hard labor, such a sentence would in no way change the conditions of existence already experienced by slaves. Thus, as Hirsch further reveals, Thomas Jefferson, who supported the sentencing of convicted people to hard labor on road and water projects, also pointed out that he would exclude slaves from this sort of punishment. Since slaves already performed hard labor, sentencing them to penal labor would not mark a difference in their condition. Jefferson suggested banishment to other countries instead.[18]

Particularly in the United States, race has always played a central role in constructing presumptions of criminality. After the abolition of slavery, former slave states passed new legislation revising the Slave Codes in order to regulate the behavior of free blacks in ways similar to those that had existed during slavery. The new Black Codes proscribed a range of actions—such as vagrancy, absence from work, breach of job contracts, the possession of firearms, and insulting gestures or acts—that were criminalized only when the person charged was black. With the passage of the Thirteenth Amendment to the Constitution, slavery and involuntary servitude were putatively abolished. However, there was a significant exception. In the wording of the amendment, slavery and involuntary servitude were abolished "except as a punishment for crime, whereof the party shall have been duly convicted." According to the Black Codes, there were crimes defined by state law for which only black people could be "duly convicted." Thus, former

slaves, who had recently been extricated from a condition of hard labor for life, could be legally sentenced to penal servitude.

In the immediate aftermath of slavery, the southern states hastened to develop a criminal justice system that could legally restrict the possibilities of freedom for newly released slaves. Black people became the prime targets of a developing convict lease system, referred to by many as a reincarnation of slavery. The Mississippi Black Codes, for example, declared vagrant "anyone/who was guilty of theft, had run away [from a job, apparently], was drunk, was wanton in conduct or speech, had neglected job or family, handled money carelessly, and . . . all other idle and disorderly persons."[19] Thus, vagrancy was coded as a black crime, one punishable by incarceration and forced labor, sometimes on the very plantations that previously had thrived on slave labor.

Mary Ellen Curtin's study of Alabama prisoners during the decades following emancipation discloses that before the four hundred thousand black slaves in that state were set free, ninety-nine percent of prisoners in Alabama's penitentiaries were white. As a consequence of the shifts provoked by the institution of the Black Codes, within a short period of time, the overwhelming majority of Alabama's convicts were black.[20] She further observes:

> Although the vast majority of Alabama's antebellum prisoners were white, the popular perception was that the South's true criminals were its black slaves. During the 1870s the growing number of black prisoners in the South further buttressed the belief that African Americans were inherently criminal and, in particular, prone to larceny.[21]

In 1883, Frederick Douglass had already written about the South's tendency to "impute crime to color."[22] When a particularly egregious crime was committed, he noted, not only was guilt frequently assigned to a black person regardless of the perpetrator's race, but white men sometimes sought to escape punishment by disguising themselves as black. Douglass would later recount one such incident that took place in Granger County, Tennessee, in which a man who appeared to be black was shot while committing a robbery. The wounded man, however, was discovered to be a respectable white citizen who had colored his face black.

The above example from Douglass demonstrates how whiteness, in the words of legal scholar Cheryl Harris, operates as property.[23] According to Harris, the fact that white identity was possessed as property meant that rights, liberties, and self-identity were affirmed for white people, while being denied to black people. The latter's only access to whiteness was through "passing." Douglass's comments indicate how this property interest in whiteness was easily reversed in schemes to deny black people their rights to due process. Interestingly, cases similar to the one Douglass discusses above emerged in the United States during the 1990s: in Boston, Charles Stuart murdered his pregnant wife and attempted to blame an anonymous black man, and in Union, South Carolina, Susan Smith killed her children and claimed they had been abducted by a black carjacker. The racialization of crime—the tendency to "impute crime to color," to use Frederick Douglass's words—did not wither away as the country became increasingly removed from slavery. Proof that crime continues to be imputed to color resides in the many evocations of "racial profiling" in our time. That it is possible to be targeted by the police for no other reason than the color of one's skin is not mere specu-

lation. Police departments in major urban areas have admitted the existence of formal procedures designed to maximize the numbers of African-Americans and Latinos arrested—even in the absence of probable cause. In the aftermath of the September 11 attacks, vast numbers of people of Middle Eastern and South Asian heritage were arrested and detained by the police agency known as Immigration and Naturalization Services (INS). The INS is the federal agency that claims the largest number of armed agents, even more than the FBI.[24]

During the post-slavery era, as black people were integrated into southern penal systems—and as the penal system became a system of penal servitude—the punishments associated with slavery became further incorporated into the penal system. "Whipping," as Matthew Mancini has observed, "was the preeminent form of punishment under slavery; and the lash, along with the chain, became the very emblem of servitude for slaves and prisoners."[25] As indicated above, black people were imprisoned under the laws assembled in the various Black Codes of the southern states, which, because they were rearticulations of the Slave Codes, tended to racialize penality and link it closely with previous regimes of slavery. The expansion of the convict lease system and the county chain gang meant that the antebellum criminal justice system, which focused far more intensely on black people than on whites, defined southern criminal justice largely as a means of controlling black labor. According to Mancini:

> Among the multifarious debilitating legacies of slavery was the conviction that blacks could only labor in a certain way—the way experience had shown them to have labored in the past: in gangs,

subjected to constant supervision, and under the discipline of the lash. Since these were the requisites of slavery, and since slaves were blacks, Southern whites almost universally concluded that blacks could not work unless subjected to such intense surveillance and discipline.[26]

Scholars who have studied the convict lease system point out that in many important respects, convict leasing was far worse than slavery, an insight that can be gleaned from titles such as *One Dies, Get Another* (by Mancini), *Worse Than Slavery* (David Oshinsky's work on Parchman Prison),[27] and *Twice the Work of Free Labor* (Alex Lichtenstein's examination of the political economy of convict leasing).[28] Slave owners may have been concerned for the survival of individual slaves, who, after all, represented significant investments. Convicts, on the other hand, were leased not as individuals, but as a group, and they could be worked literally to death without affecting the profitability of a convict crew.

According to descriptions by contemporaries, the conditions under which leased convicts and county chain gangs lived were far worse than those under which black people had lived as slaves. The records of Mississippi plantations in the Yazoo Delta during the late 1880s indicate that

the prisoners ate and slept on bare ground, without blankets or mattresses, and often without clothes. They were punished for "slow hoeing" (ten lashes), "sorry planting" (five lashes), and "being light with cotton" (five lashes). Some who attempted to escape were whipped "till the blood ran down their legs"; others had a metal spur riveted to their feet. Convicts dropped from exhaustion, pneumonia,

malaria, frostbite, consumption, sunstroke, dysentery, gunshot wounds, and "shackle poisoning" (the constant rubbing of chains and leg irons against bare flesh).[29]

The appalling treatment to which convicts were subjected under the lease system recapitulated and further extended the regimes of slavery. If, as Adam Jay Hirsch contends, the early incarnations of the U.S. penitentiary in the North tended to mirror the institution of slavery in many important respects, the post–Civil War evolution of the punishment system was in very literal ways the continuation of a slave system, which was no longer legal in the "free" world. The population of convicts, whose racial composition was dramatically transformed by the abolition of slavery, could be subjected to such intense exploitation and to such horrendous modes of punishment precisely because they continued to be perceived as slaves.

Historian Mary Ann Curtin has observed that many scholars who have acknowledged the deeply entrenched racism of the post–Civil War structures of punishment in the South have failed to identify the extent to which racism colored common-sense understandings of the circumstances surrounding the wholesale criminalization of black communities. Even antiracist historians, she contends, do not go far enough in examining the ways in which black people were made into criminals. They point out—and this, she says, is indeed partially true—that in the aftermath of emancipation large numbers of black people were forced by their new social situation to steal in order to survive. It was the transformation of petty thievery into a felony that relegated substantial numbers of black people to the "involuntary servitude" legalized by the Thirteenth Amendment. What Curtin suggests is that these

charges of theft were frequently fabricated outright. They "also served as subterfuge for political revenge. After emancipation the courtroom became an ideal place to exact racial retribution."[30] In this sense, the work of the criminal justice system was intimately related to the extralegal work of lynching. Alex Lichtenstein, whose study focuses on the role of the convict lease system in forging a new labor force for the South, identifies the lease system, along with the new Jim Crow laws, as the central institution in the development of a racial state.

> New South capitalists in Georgia and elsewhere were able to use the state to recruit and discipline a convict labor force, and thus were able to develop their states' resources without creating a wage labor force, and without undermining planters' control of black labor. In fact, quite the opposite: the penal system could be used as a powerful sanction against rural blacks who challenged the racial order upon which agricultural labor control relied.[31]

Lichtenstein discloses, for example, the extent to which the building of Georgia railroads during the nineteenth century relied on black convict labor. He further reminds us that as we drive down the most famous street in Atlanta—Peachtree Street—we ride on the backs of convicts: "[T]he renowned Peachtree Street and the rest of Atlanta's well-paved roads and modern transportation infrastructure, which helped cement its place as the commercial hub of the modern South, were originally laid by convicts."[32]

Lichtenstein's major argument is that the convict lease was not an irrational regression; it was not primarily a throwback to precapitalist modes of production. Rather, it

was a most efficient and most rational deployment of racist strategies to swiftly achieve industrialization in the South. In this sense, he argues, "convict labor was in many ways in the vanguard of the region's first tentative, ambivalent, steps toward modernity."[33]

Those of us who have had the opportunity to visit nineteenth-century mansions that were originally constructed on slave plantations are rarely content with an aesthetic appraisal of these structures, no matter how beautiful they may be. Sufficient visual imagery of toiling black slaves circulate enough in our environment for us to imagine the brutality that hides just beneath the surface of these wondrous mansions. We have learned how to recognize the role of slave labor, as well as the racism it embodied. But black convict labor remains a hidden dimension of our history. It is extremely unsettling to think of modern, industrialized urban areas as having been originally produced under the racist labor conditions of penal servitude that are often described by historians as even worse than slavery.

I grew up in the city of Birmingham, Alabama. Because of its mines—coal and iron ore—and its steel mills that remained active until the deindustrialization process of the 1980s, it was widely known as "the Pittsburgh of the South." The fathers of many of my friends worked in these mines and mills. It is only recently that I have learned that the black miners and steelworkers I knew during my childhood inherited their place in Birmingham's industrial development from black convicts forced to do this work under the lease system. As Curtin observes,

> Many ex-prisoners became miners because Alabama used prison labor extensively in its coalmines. By 1888 all of Alabama's able male prisoners were leased

to two major mining companies: the Tennessee Coal and Iron Company (TCI) and Sloss Iron and Steel Company. For a charge of up to $18.50 per month per man, these corporations "leased," or rented prison laborers and worked them in coalmines.[34]

Learning about this little-acknowledged dimension of black and labor history has caused me to reevaluate my own childhood experiences.

One of the many ruses racism achieves is the virtual erasure of historical contributions by people of color. Here we have a penal system that was racist in many respects—discriminatory arrests and sentences, conditions of work, modes of punishment—together with the racist erasure of the significant contributions made by black convicts as a result of racist coercion. Just as it is difficult to imagine how much is owed to convicts relegated to penal servitude during the nineteenth and twentieth centuries, we find it difficult today to feel a connection with the prisoners who produce a rising number of commodities that we take for granted in our daily lives. In the state of California, public colleges and universities are provided with furniture produced by prisoners, the vast majority of whom are Latino and black.

There are aspects of our history that we need to interrogate and rethink, the recognition of which may help us to adopt more complicated, critical postures toward the present and the future. I have focused on the work of a few scholars whose work urges us to raise questions about the past, present, and future. Curtin, for example, is not simply content with offering us the possibility of reexamining the place of mining and steelwork in the lives of black people in Alabama. She also uses her research to urge us to think about the uncanny parallels between the convict lease sys-

tem in the nineteenth century and prison privatization in the twenty-first.

> In the late nineteenth century, coal companies wished to keep their skilled prison laborers for as long as they could, leading to denials of "short time." Today, a slightly different economic incentive can lead to similar consequences. CCA [Corrections Corporation of America] is paid per prisoner. If the supply dries up, or too many are released too early, their profits are affected . . . Longer prison terms mean greater profits, but the larger point is that the profit motive promotes the expansion of imprisonment.[35]

The persistence of the prison as the main form of punishment, with its racist and sexist dimensions, has created this historical continuity between the nineteenth- and early-twentieth-century convict lease system and the privatized prison business today. While the convict lease system was legally abolished, its structures of exploitation have reemerged in the patterns of privatization, and, more generally, in the wide-ranging corporatization of punishment that has produced a prison industrial complex. If the prison continues to dominate the landscape of punishment throughout this century and into the next, what might await coming generations of impoverished African-Americans, Latinos, Native Americans, and Asian-Americans? Given the parallels between the prison and slavery, a productive exercise might consist in speculating about what the present might look like if slavery or its successor, the convict lease system, had not been abolished.

To be sure, I am not suggesting that the abolition of slav-

ery and the lease system has produced an era of equality and justice. On the contrary, racism surreptitiously defines social and economic structures in ways that are difficult to identify and thus are much more damaging. In some states, for example, more than one-third of black men have been labeled felons. In Alabama and Florida, once a felon, always a felon, which entails the loss of status as a rights-bearing citizen. One of the grave consequences of the powerful reach of the prison was the 2000 (s)election of George W. Bush as president. If only the black men and women denied the right to vote because of an actual or presumed felony record had been allowed to cast their ballots, Bush would not be in the White House today. And perhaps we would not be dealing with the awful costs of the War on Terrorism declared during the first year of his administration. If not for his election, the people of Iraq might not have suffered death, destruction, and environmental poisoning by U.S. military forces.

As appalling as the current political situation may be, imagine what our lives might have become if we were still grappling with the institution of slavery—or the convict lease system or racial segregation. But we do not have to speculate about living with the consequences of the prison. There is more than enough evidence in the lives of men and women who have been claimed by ever more repressive institutions and who are denied access to their families, their communities, to educational opportunities, to productive and creative work, to physical and mental recreation. And there is even more compelling evidence about the damage wrought by the expansion of the prison system in the schools located in poor communities of color that replicate the structures and regimes of the prison. When children attend schools that place a greater value on discipline and security than on knowledge and intellectual development,

they are attending prep schools for prison. If this is the predicament we face today, what might the future hold if the prison system acquires an even greater presence in our society? In the nineteenth century, antislavery activists insisted that as long as slavery continued, the future of democracy was bleak indeed. In the twenty-first century, antiprison activists insist that a fundamental requirement for the revitalization of democracy is the long-overdue abolition of the prison system.

3

Imprisonment and Reform

"One should recall that the movement for reforming the prisons, for controlling their functioning is not a recent phenomenon. It does not even seem to have originated in a recognition of failure. Prison 'reform' is virtually contemporary with the prison itself: it constitutes, as it were, its programme."

—Michel Foucault[36]

It is ironic that the prison itself was a product of concerted efforts by reformers to create a better system of punishment. If the words "prison reform" so easily slip from our lips, it is because "prison" and "reform" have been inextricably linked since the beginning of the use of imprisonment as the main means of punishing those who violate social norms. As I have already indicated, the origins of the prison are associated with the American Revolution and therefore with the resistance to the colonial power of England. Today this seems ironic, but incarceration within a penitentiary was assumed to be humane—at least far more humane than the capital and corporal punishment inherited from England and other European countries. Foucault opens his study, *Discipline and Punish: The Birth of the Prison*, with a graphic description of a 1757 execution in Paris. The man who was put to death was first forced to undergo a series of formidable tortures ordered by the court. Red-hot pincers were

pre-poison punishment! "_18th cent. punishment_"!

used to burn away the flesh from his limbs, and molten lead, boiling oil, burning resin, and other substances were melted together and poured onto the wounds. Finally, he was drawn and quartered, his body burned, and the ashes tossed into the wind.[37] Under English common law, a conviction for sodomy led to the punishment of being buried alive, and convicted heretics also were burned alive. "The crime of treason by a female was punished initially under the common law by burning alive the defendant. However, in the year 1790 this method was halted and the punishment became strangulation and burning of the corpse."[38]

European and American reformers set out to end macabre penalties such as this, as well as other forms of corporal punishment such as the stocks and pillories, whippings, brandings, and amputations. Prior to the appearance of punitive incarceration, such punishment was designed to have its most profound effect not so much on the person punished as on the crowd of spectators. Punishment was, in essence, public spectacle. Reformers such as John Howard in England and Benjamin Rush in Pennsylvania argued that punishment—if carried out in isolation, behind the walls of the prison—would cease to be revenge and would actually reform those who had broken the law.

It should also be pointed out that punishment has not been without its gendered dimensions. Women were often punished within the domestic domain, and instruments of torture were sometimes imported by authorities into the household. In seventeenth-century Britain, women whose husbands identified them as quarrelsome and unaccepting of male dominance were punished by means of a gossip's bridle, or "branks," a headpiece with a chain attached and an iron bit that was introduced into the woman's mouth.[39] Although the branking of women was often linked to a public parade, this

contraption was sometimes hooked to a wall of the house, where the punished woman remained until her husband decided to release her. I mention these forms of punishment inflicted on women because, like the punishment inflicted on slaves, they were rarely taken up by prison reformers.

Other modes of punishment that predated the rise of the prison include banishment, forced labor in galleys, transportation, and appropriation of the accused's property. The punitive transportation of large numbers of people from England, for example, facilitated the initial colonization of Australia. Transported English convicts also settled the North American colony of Georgia. During the early 1700s, one in eight transported convicts were women, and the work they were forced to perform often consisted of prostitution.[40]

Imprisonment was not employed as a principal mode of punishment until the eighteenth century in Europe and the nineteenth century in the United States. And European prison systems were instituted in Asia and Africa as an important component of colonial rule. In India, for example, the English prison system was introduced during the second half of the eighteenth century, when jails were established in the regions of Calcutta and Madras. In Europe, the penitentiary movement against capital and other corporal punishments reflected new intellectual tendencies associated with the Enlightenment, activist interventions by Protestant reformers, and structural transformations associated with the rise of industrial capitalism. In Milan in 1764, Cesare Beccaria published his *Essay on Crimes and Punishments*,[41] which was strongly influenced by notions of equality advanced by the philosophes—especially Voltaire, Rousseau, and Montesquieu. Beccaria argued that punishment should never be a private matter, nor should it be arbitrarily violent; rather, it should be public, swift, and as

lenient as possible. He revealed the contradiction of what was then a distinctive feature of imprisonment—the fact *before !* that it was generally imposed prior to the defendant's guilt or innocence being decided.

However, incarceration itself eventually became the penalty, bringing about a distinction between imprisonment as punishment and pretrial detention or detention until the infliction of punishment. The process through which imprisonment developed into the primary mode of state-inflicted punishment was very much related to the rise of capitalism and to the appearance of a new set of ideological conditions. These new conditions reflected the rise of the bourgeoisie as the social class whose interests and aspirations furthered new scientific, philosophical, cultural, and popular ideas. It is thus important to grasp the fact that the prison as we know it today did not make its appearance on the historical stage as the superior form of punishment for all times. It was simply—though we should not underestimate the complexity of this process—what made most sense at a particular moment in history. We should therefore question whether a system that was intimately related to a particular set of historical circumstances that prevailed during the eighteenth and nineteenth centuries can lay absolute claim on the twenty-first century.

It may be important at this point in our examination to acknowledge the radical shift in the social perception of the individual that appeared in the ideas of that era. With the rise of the bourgeoisie, the individual came to be regarded as a bearer of formal rights and liberties. The notion of the individual's inalienable rights and liberties was eventually memorialized in the French and American Revolution. "*Liberté, Egalité, Fraternité*" from the French Revolution and "We hold these truths to be self-evident: all men are cre-

ated equal . . ." from the American Revolution were new and radical ideas, even though they were not extended to women, workers, Africans, and Indians. Before the acceptance of the sanctity of individual rights, imprisonment could not have been understood as punishment. If the individual was not perceived as possessing inalienable rights and liberties, then the alienation of those rights and liberties by removal from society to a space tyrannically governed by the state would not have made sense. Banishment beyond the geographical limits of the town may have made sense, but not the alteration of the individual's legal status through imposition of a prison sentence.

Moreover, the prison sentence, which is always computed in terms of time, is related to abstract quantification, evoking the rise of science and what is often referred to as the Age of Reason. We should keep in mind that this was precisely the historical period when the value of labor began to be calculated in terms of time and therefore compensated in another quantifiable way, by money. The computability of state punishment in terms of time—days, months, years—resonates with the role of labor-time as the basis for computing the value of capitalist commodities. Marxist theorists of punishment have noted that precisely the historical period during which the commodity form arose is the era during which penitentiary sentences emerged as the primary form of punishment.[42]

Today, the growing social movement contesting the supremacy of global capital is a movement that directly challenges the rule of the planet—its human, animal, and plant populations, as well as its natural resources—by corporations that are primarily interested in the increased production and circulation of ever more profitable commodities. This is a challenge to the supremacy of the commodity form, a rising

resistance to the contemporary tendency to commodify every aspect of planetary existence. The question we might consider is whether this new resistance to capitalist globalization should also incorporate resistance to the prison.

Thus far I have largely used gender-neutral language to describe the historical development of the prison and its reformers. But convicts punished by imprisonment in emergent penitentiary systems were primarily male. This reflected the deeply gender-biased structure of legal, political, and economic rights. Since women were largely denied public status as rights-bearing individuals, they could not be easily punished by the deprivation of such rights through imprisonment.[43] This was especially true of married women, who had no standing before the law. According to English common law, marriage resulted in a state of "civil death," as symbolized by the wife's assumption of the husband's name. Consequently, she tended to be punished for revolting against her domestic duties rather than for failure in her meager public responsibilities. The relegation of white women to domestic economies prevented them from playing a significant role in the emergent commodity realm. This was especially true since wage labor was typically gendered as male and racialized as white. It is not fortuitous that domestic corporal punishment for women survived long after these modes of punishment had become obsolete for (white) men. The persistence of domestic violence painfully attests to these historical modes of gendered punishment.

Some scholars have argued that the word "penitentiary" may have been used first in connection with plans outlined in England in 1758 to house "penitent prostitutes." In 1777, John Howard, the leading Protestant proponent of penal reform in England, published *The State of the Prisons*,[44] in which he conceptualized imprisonment as an occasion for

religious self-reflection and self-reform. Between 1787 and 1791, the utilitarian philosopher Jeremy Bentham published his letters on a prison model he called the panopticon.[45] Bentham claimed that criminals could only internalize productive labor habits if they were under constant surveillance. According to his panopticon model, prisoners were to be housed in single cells on circular tiers, all facing a multilevel guard tower. By means of blinds and a complicated play of light and darkness, the prisoners—who would not see each other at all—would be unable to see the warden. From his vantage point, on the other hand, the warden would be able to see all of the prisoners. However—and this was the most significant aspect of Bentham's mammoth panopticon—because each individual prisoner would never be able to determine where the warden's gaze was focused, each prisoner would be compelled to act, that is, work, as if he were being watched at all times.

If we combine Howard's emphasis on disciplined self-reflection with Bentham's ideas regarding the technology of internalization designed to make surveillance and discipline the purview of the individual prisoner, we can begin to see how such a conception of the prison had far-reaching implications. The conditions of possibility for this new form of punishment were strongly anchored in a historical era during which the working class needed to be constituted as an army of self-disciplined individuals capable of performing the requisite industrial labor for a developing capitalist system.

John Howard's ideas were incorporated in the Penitentiary Act of 1799, which opened the way for the modern prison. While Jeremy Bentham's ideas influenced the development of the first national English penitentiary, located in Millbank and opened in 1816, the first full-fledged effort to create a panopticon prison was in the United States.

The Western State Penitentiary in Pittsburgh, based on a revised architectural model of the panopticon, opened in 1826. But the penitentiary had already made its appearance in the United States. Pennsylvania's Walnut Street Jail housed the first state penitentiary in the United States, when a portion of the jail was converted in 1790 from a detention facility to an institution housing convicts whose prison sentences simultaneously became punishment and occasions for penitence and reform.

Walnut Street's austere regime—total isolation in single cells where prisoners lived, ate, worked, read the Bible (if, indeed, they were literate), and supposedly reflected and repented—came to be known as the Pennsylvania system. This regime would constitute one of that era's two major models of imprisonment. Although the other model, developed in Auburn, New York, was viewed as a rival to the Pennsylvania system, the philosophical basis of the two models did not differ substantively. The Pennsylvania model, which eventually crystallized in the Eastern State Penitentiary in Cherry Hill—the plans for which were approved in 1821—emphasized total isolation, silence, and solitude, whereas the Auburn model called for solitary cells but labor in common. This mode of prison labor, which was called congregate, was supposed to unfold in total silence. Prisoners were allowed to be with each other as they worked, but only under condition of silence. Because of its more efficient labor practices, Auburn eventually became the dominant model, both for the United States and Europe.

Why would eighteenth- and nineteenth-century reformers become so invested in creating conditions of punishment based on solitary confinement? Today, aside from death, solitary confinement—next to torture, or as a form of torture—is considered the worst form of punishment imagina-

ble. Then, however, it was assumed to have an emancipatory effect. The body was placed in conditions of segregation and solitude in order to allow the soul to flourish. It is not accidental that most of the reformers of that era were deeply religious and therefore saw the architecture and regimes of the penitentiary as emulating the architecture and regimes of monastic life. Still, observers of the new penitentiary saw, early on, the real potential for insanity in solitary confinement. In an often-quoted passage of his *American Notes*, Charles Dickens prefaced a description of his 1842 visit to Eastern Penitentiary with the observation that "the system here is rigid, strict, and hopeless solitary confinement. I believe it, in its effects, to be cruel and wrong."

> In its intention I am well convinced that it is kind, humane, and meant for reformation; but I am persuaded that those who devised this system of Prison Discipline, and those benevolent gentlemen who carry it into execution, do not know what it is that they are doing. I believe that very few men are capable of estimating the immense amount of torture and agony that this dreadful punishment, prolonged for years, inflicts upon the sufferers . . . I am only the more convinced that there is a depth of terrible endurance in it which none but the sufferers themselves can fathom, and which no man has a right to inflict upon his fellow-creature. I hold this slow and daily tampering with the mysteries of the brain to be immeasurably worse than any torture of the body . . . because its wounds are not upon the surface, and it extorts few cries that human ears can hear; therefore I the more denounce it, as a secret punishment which slumbering humanity is not roused up to stay.[46]

Unlike other Europeans such as Alexis de Tocqueville and Gustave de Beaumont, who believed that such punishment would result in moral renewal and thus mold convicts into better citizens,[47] Dickens was of the opinion that "[t]hose who have undergone this punishment MUST pass into society again morally unhealthy and diseased."[48] This early critique of the penitentiary and its regime of solitary confinement troubles the notion that imprisonment is the most suitable form of punishment for a democratic society.

The current construction and expansion of state and federal super-maximum security prisons, whose putative purpose is to address disciplinary problems within the penal system, draws upon the historical conception of the penitentiary, then considered the most progressive form of punishment. Today African-Americans and Latinos are vastly overrepresented in these supermax prisons and control units, the first of which emerged when federal correctional authorities began to send prisoners housed throughout the system whom they deemed to be "dangerous" to the federal prison in Marion, Illinois. In 1983, the entire prison was "locked down," which meant that prisoners were confined to their cells twenty-three hours a day. This lockdown became permanent, thus furnishing the general model for the control unit and supermax prison.[49] Today, there are approximately sixty super-maximum security federal and state prisons located in thirty-six states and many more supermax units in virtually every state in the country.

A description of supermaxes in a 1997 Human Rights Watch report sounds chillingly like Dickens's description of Eastern State Penitentiary. What is different, however, is that all references to individual rehabilitation have disappeared.

Inmates in super-maximum security facilities are usually held in single cell lock-down, commonly referred to as solitary confinement . . . [C]ongregate activities with other prisoners are usually prohibited; other prisoners cannot even be seen from an inmate's cell; communication with other prisoners is prohibited or difficult (consisting, for example, of shouting from cell to cell); visiting and telephone privileges are limited.[50]

The new generation of super-maximum security facilities also rely on state-of-the-art technology for monitoring and controlling prisoner conduct and movement, utilizing, for example, video monitors and remote-controlled electronic doors.[51] "These prisons represent the application of sophisticated, modern technology dedicated entirely to the task of social control, and they isolate, regulate and surveil more effectively than anything that has preceded them."[52]

I have highlighted the similarities between the early U.S. penitentiary—with its aspirations toward individual rehabilitation—and the repressive supermaxes of our era as a reminder of the mutability of history. What was once regarded as progressive and even revolutionary represents today the marriage of technological superiority and political backwardness. No one—not even the most ardent defenders of the supermax—would try to argue today that absolute segregation, including sensory deprivation, is restorative and healing. The prevailing justification for the supermax is that the horrors it creates are the perfect complement for the horrifying personalities deemed the worst of the worst by the prison system. In other words, there is no pretense that rights are respected, there is no concern for the individual, there is no sense that men and women incarcerated in super-

maxes deserve anything approaching respect and comfort. According to a 1999 report issued by the National Institute of Corrections,

> Generally, the overall constitutionality of these [supermax] programs remains unclear. As larger numbers of inmates with a greater diversity of characteristics, backgrounds, and behaviors are incarcerated in these facilities, the likelihood of legal challenge is increased.[53]

During the eighteenth and nineteenth centuries, absolute solitude and strict regimentation of the prisoner's every action were viewed as strategies for transforming habits and ethics. That is to say, the idea that imprisonment should be the main form of punishment reflected a belief in the potential of white mankind for progress, not only in science and industry, but at the level of the individual member of society as well. Prison reformers mirrored Enlightenment assumptions of progress in every aspect of human—or to be more precise, white Western—society. In his 1987 study *Imagining the Penitentiary: Fiction and the Architecture of Mind in Eighteenth-Century England*, John Bender proposes the very intriguing argument that the emergent literary genre of the novel furthered a discourse of progress and individual transformation that encouraged attitudes toward punishment to change.[54] These attitudes, he suggests, heralded the conception and construction of penitentiary prisons during the latter part of the eighteenth century as a reform suited to the capacities of those who were deemed human.

Reformers who called for the imposition of penitentiary architecture and regimes on the then existing structure of the prison aimed their critiques at the prisons that were primari-

ly used for purposes of pretrial detention or as an alternative punishment for those who were unable to pay fines exacted by the courts. John Howard, the most well known of these reformers, was what you might today call a prison activist. Beginning in 1773, at the age of forty-seven, he initiated a series of visits that took him "to every institution for the poor in Europe . . . [a campaign] which cost him his fortune and finally his life in a typhus war of the Russian army at Cherson in 1791."[55] At the conclusion of his first trip abroad, he successfully ran for the office of sheriff in Bedfordshire. As sheriff he investigated the prisons under his own jurisdiction and later "set out to visit every prison in England and Wales to document the evils he had first observed at Bedford."[56]

Bender argues that the novel helped facilitate these campaigns to transform the old prisons—which were filthy and in disarray, and which thrived on the bribery of the wardens—into well-ordered rehabilitative penitentiaries. He shows that novels such as *Moll Flanders* and *Robinson Crusoe* emphasized "the power of confinement to reshape personality"[57] and popularized some of the ideas that moved reformers to action. As Bender points out, the eighteenth-century reformers criticized the old prisons for their chaos, their lack of organization and classification, for the easy circulation of alcohol and prostitution they permitted, and for the prevalence of contagion and disease.

The reformers, primarily Protestant, among whom Quakers were especially dominant, couched their ideas in large part in religious frameworks. Though John Howard was not himself a Quaker—he was an independent Protestant—nevertheless

> [h]e was drawn to Quaker asceticism and adopted the dress "of a plain Friend." His own brand of piety

was strongly reminiscent of the Quaker traditions of silent prayer, "suffering" introspection, and faith in the illumining power of God's light. Quakers, for their part, were bound to be drawn to the idea of imprisonment as a purgatory, as a forced withdrawal from the distractions of the senses into silent and solitary confrontation with the self. Howard conceived of a convict's process of reformation in terms similar to the spiritual awakening of a believer at a Quaker meeting.[58]

However, according to Michael Ignatieff, Howard's contributions did not so much reside in the religiosity of his reform efforts.

> The originality of Howard's indictment lies in its "scientific," not in its moral character. Elected a Fellow of the Royal Society in 1756 and author of several scientific papers on climatic variations in Bedfordshire, Howard was one of the first philanthropists to attempt a systematic statistical description of a social problem.[59]

Likewise, Bender's analysis of the relationship between the novel and the penitentiary emphasizes the extent to which the philosophical underpinnings of the prison reformer's campaigns echoed the materialism and utilitarianism of the English Enlightenment. The campaign to reform the prisons was a project to impose order, classification, cleanliness, good work habits, and self-consciousness. He argues that people detained within the old prisons were not severely restricted—they sometimes even enjoyed the freedom to move in and out of the prison. They were not

compelled to work and, depending on their own resources, could eat and drink as they wished. Even sex was sometimes available, as prostitutes were sometimes allowed temporary entrance into the prisons. Howard and other reformers called for the imposition of rigid rules that would "enforce solitude and penitence, cleanliness and work."[60]

"The new penitentiaries," according to Bender, "supplanting both the old prisons and houses of correction, explicitly reached toward . . . three goals: maintenance of order within a largely urban labor force, salvation of the soul, and rationalization of personality."[61] He argues that this is precisely what was narratively accomplished by the novel. It ordered and classified social life, it represented individuals as conscious of their surroundings and as self-aware and self-fashioning. Bender thus sees a kinship between two major developments of the eighteenth century—the rise of the novel in the cultural sphere and the rise of the penitentiary in the socio-legal sphere. If the novel as a cultural form helped to produce the penitentiary, then prison reformers must have been influenced by the ideas generated by and through the eighteenth-century novel.

Literature has continued to play a role in campaigns around the prison. During the twentieth century, prison writing, in particular, has periodically experienced waves of popularity. The public recognition of prison writing in the United States has historically coincided with the influence of social movements calling for prison reform and/or abolition. Robert Burns's *I Am a Fugitive from a Georgia Chain Gang*,[62] and the 1932 Hollywood film upon which it was based, played a central role in the campaign to abolish the chain gang. During the 1970s, which were marked by intense organizing within, outside, and across prison walls, numerous works authored by prisoners followed the 1970 publica-

tion of George Jackson's *Soledad Brother* and the antholo-gy I coedited with Bettina Aptheker, *If They Come in the Morning*.[64] While many prison writers during that era had discovered the emancipatory potential of writing on their own, relying either on the education they had received prior to their imprisonment or on their tenacious efforts at self-education, others pursued their writing as a direct result of the expansion of prison educational programs during that era. Mumia Abu-Jamal, who has challenged the contemporary dismantling of prison education programs, asks in *Live from Death Row*,

> What societal interest is served by prisoners who remain illiterate? What social benefit is there in ignorance? How are people corrected while impris-oned if their education is outlawed? Who profits (other than the prison establishment itself) from stupid prisoners?[65]

A practicing journalist before his arrest in 1982 on charges of killing Philadelphia policeman Daniel Faulkner, Abu-Jamal has regularly produced articles on capital punishment, focusing especially on its racial and class disproportions. His ideas have helped to link critiques of the death penalty with the more general challenges to the expanding U.S. prison sys-tem and are particularly helpful to activists who seek to asso-ciate death penalty abolitionism with prison abolitionism. His prison writings have been published in both popular and scholarly journals (such as *The Nation* and *Yale Law Journal*) as well as in three collections, *Live from Death Row*, *Death Blossoms*,[66] and *All Things Censored*.[67]

Abu-Jamal and many other prison writers have strongly criticized the prohibition of Pell Grants for prisoners, which

was enacted in the 1994 crime bill,[68] as indicative of the contemporary pattern of dismantling educational programs behind bars. As creative writing courses for prisoners were defunded, virtually every literary journal publishing prisoners' writing eventually collapsed. Of the scores of magazines and newspapers produced behind walls, only the *Angolite* at Louisiana's Angola Prison and *Prison Legal News* at Washington State Prison remain. What this means is that precisely at a time of consolidating a significant writing culture behind bars, repressive strategies are being deployed to dissuade prisoners from educating themselves.

If the publication of Malcolm X's autobiography marks a pivotal moment in the development of prison literature and a moment of vast promise for prisoners who try to make education a major dimension of their time behind bars,[69] contemporary prison practices are systematically dashing those hopes. In the 1950s, Malcolm's prison education was a dramatic example of prisoners' ability to turn their incarceration into a transformative experience. With no available means of organizing his quest for knowledge, he proceeded to read a dictionary, copying each word in his own hand. By the time he could immerse himself in reading, he noted, "months passed without my even thinking about being imprisoned. In fact, up to then, I never had been so truly free in my life."[70] Then, according to Malcolm, prisoners who demonstrated an unusual interest in reading were assumed to have embarked upon a journey of self-rehabilitation and were frequently allowed special privileges—such as checking out more than the maximum number of books. Even so, in order to pursue this self-education, Malcolm had to work against the prison regime—he often read on his cell floor, long after lights-out, by the glow of the corridor light, taking care to return to bed each

hour for the two minutes during which the guard marched past his cell.

The contemporary disestablishment of writing and other prison educational programs is indicative of the official disregard today for rehabilitative strategies, particularly those that encourage individual prisoners to acquire autonomy of the mind. The documentary film *The Last Graduation* describes the role prisoners played in establishing a four-year college program at New York's Greenhaven Prison and, twenty-two years later, the official decision to dismantle it. According to Eddie Ellis, who spent twenty-five years in prison and is currently a well-known leader of the antiprison movement, "As a result of Attica, college programs came into the prisons."[71]

In the aftermath of the 1971 prisoner rebellion at Attica and the government-sponsored massacre, public opinion began to favor prison reform. Forty-three Attica prisoners and eleven guards and civilians were killed by the National Guard, who had been ordered to retake the prison by Governor Nelson Rockefeller. The leaders of the prison rebellion had been very specific about their demands. In their "practical demands" they expressed concerns about diet, improvement in the quality of guards, more realistic rehabilitation programs, and better education programs. They also wanted religious freedom, freedom to engage in political activity, and an end to censorship—all of which they saw as indispensable to their educational needs. As Eddie Ellis observes in *The Last Graduation*,

> Prisoners very early recognized the fact that they needed to be better educated, that the more education they had, the better they would be able to deal with themselves and their problems, the problems

of the prisons and the problems of the communities from which most of them came.

Lateef Islam, another former prisoner featured in this documentary, said, "We held classes before the college came. We taught each other, and sometimes under penalty of a beat-up."

After the Attica Rebellion, more than five hundred prisoners were transferred to Greenhaven, including some of the leaders who continued to press for educational programs. As a direct result of their demands, Marist College, a New York state college near Greenhaven, began to offer college-level courses in 1973 and eventually established the infrastructure for an on-site four-year college program. The program thrived for twenty-two years. Some of the many prisoners who earned their degrees at Greenhaven pursued postgraduate studies after their release. As the documentary powerfully demonstrates, the program produced dedicated men who left prison and offered their newly acquired knowledge and skills to their communities on the outside.

In 1994, consistent with the general pattern of creating more prisons and more repression within all prisons, Congress took up the question of withdrawing college funding for inmates. The congressional debate concluded with a decision to add an amendment to the 1994 crime bill that eliminated all Pell Grants for prisoners, thus effectively defunding all higher educational programs. After twenty-two years, Marist College was compelled to terminate its program at Greenhaven Prison. Thus, the documentary revolves around the very last graduation ceremony on July 15, 1995, and the poignant process of removing the books that, in many ways, symbolized the possibilities of freedom. Or, as one of the Marist professors said, "They see books as

full of gold." The prisoner who for many years had served as a clerk for the college sadly reflected, as books were being moved, that there was nothing left to do in prison—except perhaps bodybuilding. "But," he asked, "what's the use of building your body if you can't build your mind?" Ironically, not long after educational programs were disestablished, weights and bodybuilding equipment were also removed from most U.S. prisons.

4

How Gender Structures the Prison System

"I have been told that I will never leave prison if I continue to fight the system. My answer is that one must be alive in order to leave prison, and our current standard of medical care is tantamount to a death sentence. Therefore, I have no choice but to continue . . . Conditions within the institution continually reinvoke memories of violence and oppression, often with devastating results. Unlike other incarcerated women who have come forward to reveal their impressions of prison, I do not feel 'safer' here because 'the abuse has stopped.' *It has not stopped.* It has shifted shape and paced itself differently, but it is as insidious and pervasive in prison as ever it was in the world I know outside these walls. What has ceased is my ignorance of the facts concerning abuse—and my willingness to tolerate it in silence."

—Marcia Bunny[72]

Over the last five years, the prison system has received far more attention by the media than at any time since the period following the 1971 Attica Rebellion. However, with a few important exceptions, women have been left out of the public discussions about the expansion of the U.S. prison system. I am not suggesting that simply bringing women into the existing conversations on jails and prisons will deepen

our analysis of state punishment and further the project of prison abolition. Addressing issues that are specific to women's prisons is of vital importance, but it is equally important to shift the way we think about the prison system as a whole. Certainly women's prison practices are gendered, but so, too, are men's prison practices. To assume that men's institutions constitute the norm and women's institutions are marginal is, in a sense, to participate in the very normalization of prisons that an abolitionist approach seeks to contest. Thus, the title of this chapter is not "Women and the Prison System," but rather "How Gender Structures the Prison System." Moreover, scholars and activists who are involved in feminist projects should not consider the structure of state punishment as marginal to their work. Forward-looking research and organizing strategies should recognize that the deeply gendered character of punishment both reflects and further entrenches the gendered structure of the larger society.

Women prisoners have produced a small but impressive body of literature that has illuminated significant aspects of the organization of punishment that would have otherwise remained unacknowledged. Assata Shakur's memoirs,[73] for example, reveal the dangerous intersections of racism, male domination, and state strategies of political repression. In 1977 she was convicted on charges of murder and assault in connection with a 1973 incident that left one New Jersey state trooper dead and another wounded. She and her companion, Zayd Shakur, who was killed during the shootout, were the targets of what we now name racial profiling and were stopped by state troopers under the pretext of a broken taillight. At the time Assata Shakur, known then as Joanne Chesimard, was underground and had been anointed by the police and the media as the "Soul of the Black Liberation

Army." By her 1977 conviction, she either had been acquitted or had charges dismissed in six other cases—upon the basis of which she had been declared a fugitive in the first place. Her attorney, Lennox Hinds, has pointed out that since it was proven that Assata Shakur did not handle the gun with which the state troopers were shot, her mere presence in the automobile, against the backdrop of the media demonization to which she was subjected, constituted the basis of her conviction. In the foreword to Shakur's autobiography Hinds writes:

> In the history of New Jersey, no woman pretrial detainee or prisoner has ever been treated as she was, continuously confined in a men's prison, under twenty-four-hour surveillance of her most intimate functions, without intellectual sustenance, adequate medical attention, and exercise, and without the company of other women for all the years she was in their custody.[74]

There is no doubt that Assata Shakur's status as a black political prisoner accused of killing a state trooper caused her to be singled out by the authorities for unusually cruel treatment. However, her own account emphasizes the extent to which her individual experiences reflected those of other imprisoned women, especially black and Puerto Rican women. Her description of the strip search, which focuses on the internal examination of body cavities, is especially revealing:

> Joan Bird and Afeni Shakur [members of the Black Panther Party] had told me about it after they had been bailed out in the Panther 21 trial. When they had told me, I was horrified.

"You mean they really put their hands inside you, to search you?" I had asked.

"Uh-huh," they answered. Every woman who has ever been on the rock, or in the old house of detention, can tell you about it. The women call it "getting the finger" or, more vulgarly, "getting finger-fucked."

"What happens if you refuse?" I had asked Afeni.

"They lock you in the hole and they don't let you out until you consent to be searched internally."

I thought about refusing, but I sure as hell didn't want to be in the hole. I had had enough of solitary. The "internal search" was as humiliating and disgusting as it sounded. You sit on the edge of this table and the nurse holds your legs open and sticks a finger in your vagina and moves it around. She has a plastic glove on. Some of them try to put one finger in your vagina and another one up your rectum at the same time.[5]

I have quoted this passage so extensively because it exposes an everyday routine in women's prisons that verges on sexual assault as much as it is taken for granted. Having been imprisoned in the Women's House of Detention to which Joan Bird and Afeni Shakur refer, I can personally affirm the veracity of their claims. Over thirty years after Bird and Afeni Shakur were released and after I myself spent several months in the Women's House of Detention, this issue of the strip search is still very much on the front burner of women's prison activism. In 2001 Sisters Inside, an Australian support organization for women prisoners, launched a national campaign against the strip search, the slogan of which was "Stop State Sexual Assault." Assata

Shakur's autobiography provides an abundance of insights about the gendering of state punishment and reveals the extent to which women's prisons have held on to oppressive patriarchal practices that are considered obsolete in the "free world." She spent six years in several jails and prisons before escaping in 1979 and receiving political asylum by the Republic of Cuba in 1984, where she lives today.

Elizabeth Gurley Flynn wrote an earlier account of life in a women's prison, *The Alderson Story: My Life as a Political Prisoner*.[76] At the height of the McCarthy era, Flynn, a labor activist and Communist leader, was convicted under the Smith Act and served two years in Alderson Federal Reformatory for Women from 1955 to 1957. Following the dominant model for women's prisons during that period, Alderson's regimes were based on the assumption that "criminal" women could be rehabilitated by assimilating correct womanly behaviors—that is, by becoming experts in domesticity—especially cooking, cleaning, and sewing. Of course, training designed to produce better wives and mothers among middle-class white women effectively produced skilled domestic servants among black and poor women. Flynn's book provides vivid descriptions of these everyday regimes. Her autobiography is located in a tradition of prison writing by political prisoners that also includes women of this era. Contemporary writings by women political prisoners today include poems and short stories by Ericka Huggins and Susan Rosenberg, analyses of the prison industrial complex by Linda Evans, and curricula for HIV/AIDS education in women's prisons by Kathy Boudin and the members of the Bedford Hills ACE collective.[77]

Despite the availability of perceptive portrayals of life in women's prisons, it has been extremely difficult to persuade the public—and even, on occasion, to persuade prison

activists who are primarily concerned with the plight of male prisoners—of the centrality of gender to an understanding of state punishment. Although men constitute the vast majority of prisoners in the world, important aspects of the operation of state punishment are missed if it is assumed that women are marginal and thus undeserving of attention. The most frequent justification for the inattention to women prisoners and to the particular issues surrounding women's imprisonment is the relatively small proportion of women among incarcerated populations throughout the world. In most countries, the percentage of women among prison populations hovers around five percent.[8] However, the economic and political shifts of the 1980s—the globalization of economic markets, the deindustrialization of the U.S. economy, the dismantling of such social service programs as Aid to Families of Dependent Children, and, of course, the prison construction boom—produced a significant acceleration in the rate of women's imprisonment both inside and outside the United States. In fact, women remain today the fastest-growing sector of the U.S. prison population. This recent rise in the rate of women's imprisonment points directly to the economic context that produced the prison industrial complex and that has had a devastating impact on men and women alike.

It is from this perspective of the contemporary expansion of prisons, both in the United States and throughout the world, that we should examine some of the historical and ideological aspects of state punishment imposed on women. Since the end of the eighteenth century, when, as we have seen, imprisonment began to emerge as the dominant form of punishment, convicted women have been represented as essentially different from their male counterparts. It is true that men who commit the kinds of transgressions that are

regarded as punishable by the state are labeled as social deviants. Nevertheless, masculine criminality has always been deemed more "normal" than feminine criminality. There has always been a tendency to regard those women who have been publicly punished by the state for their misbehaviors as significantly more aberrant and far more threatening to society than their numerous male counterparts.

In seeking to understand this gendered difference in the perception of prisoners, it should be kept in mind that as the prison emerged and evolved as the major form of public punishment, women continued to be routinely subjected to forms of punishment that have not been acknowledged as such. For example, women have been incarcerated in psychiatric institutions in greater proportions than in prisons.[79] Studies indicating that women have been even more likely to end up in mental facilities than men suggest that while jails and prisons have been dominant institutions for the control of men, mental institutions have served a similar purpose for women. That is, deviant men have been constructed as criminal, while deviant women have been constructed as insane. Regimes that reflect this assumption continue to inform the women's prison. Psychiatric drugs continue to be distributed far more extensively to imprisoned women than to their male counterparts. A Native American woman incarcerated in the Women's Correctional Center in Montana related her experience with psychotropic drugs to sociologist Luana Ross:

> Haldol is a drug they give people who can't cope with lockup. It makes you feel dead, paralyzed. And then I started getting side effects from Haldol. I wanted to fight anybody, any of the officers. I was screaming at them and telling them to get out of

use of drugs to control

my face, so the doctor said, "We can't have that." And, they put me on Tranxene. I don't take pills; I never had trouble sleeping until I got here. Now I'm supposed to see [the counselor] again because of my dreams. If you got a problem, they're not going to take care of it. They're going to put you on drugs so they can control you.[80]

Prior to the emergence of the penitentiary and thus of the notion of punishment as "doing time," the use of confinement to control beggars, thieves, and the insane did not necessarily distinguish among these categories of deviancy. At this phase in the history of punishment—prior to the American and French Revolutions—the classification process through which criminality is differentiated from poverty and mental illness had not yet developed. As the discourse on criminality and the corresponding institutions to control it distinguished the "criminal" from the "insane," the gendered distinction took hold and continued to structure penal policies. Gendered as female, this category of insanity was highly sexualized. When we consider the impact of class and race here, we can say that for white and affluent women, this equalization tends to serve as evidence for emotional and mental disorders, but for black and poor women, it has pointed to criminality.

It should also be kept in mind that until the abolition of slavery, the vast majority of black women were subject to regimes of punishment that differed significantly from those experienced by white women. As slaves, they were directly and often brutally disciplined for conduct considered perfectly normal in a context of freedom. Slave punishment was visibly gendered—special penalties, were, for example, reserved for pregnant women unable to reach the quotas that

determined how long and how fast they should work. In the slave narrative of Moses Grandy, an especially brutal form of whipping is described in which the woman was required to lie on the ground with her stomach positioned in a hole, whose purpose was to safeguard the fetus (conceived as future slave labor). If we expand our definition of punishment under slavery, we can say that the coerced sexual relations between slave and master constituted a penalty exacted on women, if only for the sole reason that they were slaves. In other words, the deviance of the slave master was transferred to the slave woman, whom he victimized. Likewise, sexual abuse by prison guards is translated into hypersexuality of women prisoners. The notion that female "deviance" always has a sexual dimension persists in the contemporary era, and this intersection of criminality and sexuality continues to be racialized. Thus, white women labeled as "criminals" are more closely associated with blackness than their "normal" counterparts.

Prior to the emergence of the prison as the major form of public punishment, it was taken for granted that violators of the law would be subjected to corporal and frequently capital penalties. What is not generally recognized is the connection between state-inflicted corporal punishment and the physical assaults on women in domestic spaces. This form of bodily discipline has continued to be routinely meted out to women in the context of intimate relationships, but it is rarely understood to be related to state punishment.

Quaker reformers in the United States—especially the Philadelphia Society for Alleviating the Miseries of Public Prisons, founded in 1787—played a pivotal role in campaigns to substitute imprisonment for corporal punishment. Following in the tradition established by Elizabeth Fry in England, Quakers were also responsible for extended crusades

to institute separate prisons for women. Given the practice of incarcerating criminalized women in men's prisons, the demand for separate women's prisons was viewed as quite radical during this period. Fry formulated principles governing prison reform for women in her 1827 work, *Observations in Visiting, Superintendence and Government of Female Prisoners*, which were taken up in the United States by women such as Josephine Shaw Lowell and Abby Hopper Gibbons. In the 1870s, Lowell and Gibbons helped to lead the campaign in New York for separate prisons for women.

Prevailing attitudes toward women convicts differed from those toward men convicts, who were assumed to have forfeited rights and liberties that women generally could not claim even in the "free world." Although some women were housed in penitentiaries, the institution itself was gendered as male, for by and large no particular arrangements were made to accommodate sentenced women.

> The women who served in penal institutions between 1820 and 1870 were not subject to the prison reform experienced by male inmates. Officials employed isolation, silence, and hard labor to rehabilitate male prisoners. The lack of accommodations for female inmates made isolation and silence impossible for them and productive labor was not considered an important part of their routine. The neglect of female prisoners, however, was rarely benevolent. Rather, a pattern of overcrowding, harsh treatment, and sexual abuse recurred throughout prison histories.[81]

Male punishment was linked ideologically to penitence and reform. The very forfeiture of rights and liberties implied

that with self-reflection, religious study, and work, male convicts could achieve redemption and could recover these rights and liberties. However, since women were not acknowledged as securely in possession of these rights, they were not eligible to participate in this process of redemption.

According to dominant views, women convicts were irrevocably fallen women, with no possibility of salvation. If male criminals were considered to be public individuals who had simply violated the social contract, female criminals were seen as having transgressed fundamental moral principles of womanhood. The reformers, who, following Elizabeth Fry, argued that women were capable of redemption, did not really contest these ideological assumptions about women's place. In other words, they did not question the very notion of "fallen women." Rather, they simply opposed the idea that "fallen women" could not be saved. They could be saved, the reformers contended, and toward that end they advocated separate penal facilities and a specifically female approach to punishment. Their approach called for architectural models that replaced cells with cottages and "rooms" in a way that was supposed to infuse domesticity into prison life. This model facilitated a regime devised to reintegrate criminalized women into the domestic life of wife and mother. They did not, however, acknowledge the class and race underpinnings of this regime. Training that was, on the surface, designed to produce good wives and mothers in effect steered poor women (and especially black women) into "free world" jobs in domestic service. Instead of stay-at-home skilled wives and mothers, many women prisoners, upon release, would become maids, cooks, and washerwomen for more affluent women. A female custodial staff, the reformers also argued, would minimize the sexual temptations, which they believed were often at the root of female criminality.

When the reform movement calling for separate prisons for women emerged in England and the United States during the nineteenth century, Elizabeth Fry, Josephine Shaw, and other advocates argued against the established idea that criminal women were beyond the reach of moral rehabilitation. Like male convicts, who presumably could be "corrected" by rigorous prison regimes, female convicts, they suggested, could also be molded into moral beings by differently gendered imprisonment regimes. Architectural changes, domestic regimes, and an all-female custodial staff were implemented in the reformatory program proposed by reformers,[82] and eventually women's prisons became as strongly anchored to the social landscape as men's prisons, but even more invisible. Their greater invisibility was as much a reflection of the way women's domestic duties under patriarchy were assumed to be normal, natural, and consequently invisible as it was of the relatively small numbers of women incarcerated in these new institutions.

Twenty-one years after the first English reformatory for women was established in London in 1853, the first U.S. reformatory for women was opened in Indiana. The aim was to

> train the prisoners in the "important" female role of domesticity. Thus an important role of the reform movement in women's prisons was to encourage and ingrain "appropriate" gender roles, such as vocational training in cooking, sewing and cleaning. To accommodate these goals, the reformatory cottages were usually designed with kitchens, living rooms, and even some nurseries for prisoners with infants.[83]

However, this feminized public punishment did not affect all women in the same way. When black and Native American women were imprisoned in reformatories, they often were segregated from white women. Moreover, they tended to be disproportionately sentenced to men's prisons. In the southern states in the aftermath of the Civil War, black women endured the cruelties of the convict lease system unmitigated by the feminization of punishment; neither their sentences nor the labor they were compelled to do were lessened by virtue of their gender. As the U.S. prison system evolved during the twentieth century, feminized modes of punishment—the cottage system, domestic training, and so on—were designed ideologically to reform white women, relegating women of color in large part to realms of public punishment that made no pretense of offering them femininity.

Moreover, as Lucia Zedner has pointed out, sentencing practices for women within the reformatory system often required women of all racial backgrounds to do more time than men for similar offenses. "This differential was justified on the basis that women were sent to reformatories not to be punished in proportion to the seriousness of their offense but to be reformed and retrained, a process that, it was argued, required time."[84] At the same time, Zedner points out, this tendency to send women to prison for longer terms than men was accelerated by the eugenics movement, "which sought to have 'genetically inferior' women removed from social circulation for as many of their childbearing years as possible."[85]

At the beginning of the twenty-first century, women's prisons have begun to look more like their male counterparts, particularly facilities constructed in the contemporary era of the prison industrial complex. As corporate involvement in punishment expands in ways that would have been

unimaginable just two decades ago, the prison's presumed goal of rehabilitation has been thoroughly displaced by incapacitation as the major objective of imprisonment. As I have already pointed out, now that the population of U.S. prisons and jails has surpassed two million people, the rate of increase in the numbers of women prisoners has exceeded that of men. As criminologist Elliot Currie has pointed out,

> For most of the period after World War II, the female incarceration rate hovered at around 8 per 100,000; it did not reach double digits until 1977. Today it is 51 per 100,000 . . . At the current rates of increase, there will be more women in American prisons in the year 2010 than there were inmates of both sexes in 1970. When we combine the effects of race and gender, the nature of these shifts in the prison population is even clearer. The prison incarceration rate for black women today exceeds that for white *men* as recently as 1980.[86]

Luana Ross's study of Native American women incarcerated in the Women's Correctional Center in Montana argues that "prisons, as employed by the Euro-American system, operate to keep Native Americans in a colonial situation."[87] She points out that Native people are vastly overrepresented in the country's federal and state prisons. In Montana, where she did her research, they constitute 6 percent of the general population, but 17.3 percent of the imprisoned population. Native women are even more disproportionately present in Montana's prison system. They constitute 25 percent of all women imprisoned by the state.[88]

Thirty years ago, around the time of the Attica uprising and the murder of George Jackson at San Quentin, radical

opposition to the prison system identified it as a principal site of state violence and repression. In part as a reaction to the invisibility of women prisoners in this movement and in part as a consequence of the rising women's liberation movement, specific campaigns developed in defense of the rights of women prisoners. Many of these campaigns put forth—and continue to advance—radical critiques of state repression and violence. Within the correctional community, however, feminism has been influenced largely by liberal constructions of gender equality.

In contrast to the nineteenth-century reform movement, which was grounded in an ideology of gender difference, late-twentieth-century "reforms" have relied on a "separate but equal" model. This "separate but equal" approach often has been applied uncritically, ironically resulting in demands for more repressive conditions in order to render women's facilities "equal" to men's. A clear example of this can be discovered in a memoir, *The Warden Wore Pink*, written by a former warden of Huron Valley Women's Prison in Michigan. During the 1980s, the author, Tekla Miller, advocated a change in policies within the Michigan correctional system that would result in women prisoners being treated *the same* as men prisoners. With no trace of irony, she characterizes as "feminist" her own fight for "gender equality" between male and female prisoners and for equality between male and female institutions of incarceration. One of these campaigns focuses on the unequal allocation of weapons, which she sought to remedy:

> Arsenals in men's prisons are large rooms with shelves of shotguns, rifles, hand guns, ammunition, gas canisters, and riot equipment . . . Huron Valley Women's arsenal was a small, five feet by two feet

closet that held two rifles, eight shotguns, two bull-horns, five handguns, four gas canisters, and twenty sets of restraints.[89]

It does not occur to her that a more productive version of feminism would also question the organization of state punishment for men as well and, in my opinion, would seriously consider the proposition that the institution as a whole—gendered as it is—calls for the kind of critique that might lead us to consider its abolition.

Miller also describes the case of an attempted escape by a woman prisoner. The prisoner climbed over the razor ribbon but was captured after she jumped to the ground on the other side. This escape attempt occasioned a debate about the disparate treatment of men and women escapees. Miller's position was that guards should be instructed to shoot at women just as they were instructed to shoot at men. She argued that parity for women and men prisoners should consist in their equal right to be fired upon by guards. The outcome of the debate, Miller observed, was that

escaping women prisoners in medium or higher [security] prisons are treated the same way as men. A warning shot is fired. If the prisoner fails to halt and is over the fence, an officer is allowed to shoot to injure. If the officer's life is in danger, the officer can shoot to kill.[90]

Paradoxically, demands for parity with men's prisons, instead of creating greater educational, vocational, and health opportunities for women prisoners, often have led to more repressive conditions for women. This is not only a consequence of deploying liberal—that is, formalistic—

notions of equality, but of, more dangerous, allowing male prisons to function as the punishment norm. Miller points out that she attempted to prevent a female prisoner, whom she characterizes as a "murderer" serving a long term, from participating in graduation ceremonies at the University of Michigan because male murderers were not given such privileges. (Of course, she does not indicate the nature of the woman's murder charges—whether, for instance, she was convicted of killing an abusive partner, as is the case for a substantial number of women convicted of murder.) Although Miller did not succeed in preventing the inmate from participating in the commencement, in addition to her cap and gown, the prisoner was made to wear leg chains and handcuffs during the ceremony.[91] This is indeed a bizarre example of feminist demands for equality within the prison system.

A widely publicized example of the use of repressive paraphernalia historically associated with the treatment of male prisoners to create "equality" for female prisoners was the 1996 decision by Alabama's prison commissioner to establish women's chain gangs. After Alabama became the first state to reinstitute chain gangs in 1995, then State Corrections Commissioner Ron Jones announced the following year that women would be shackled while they cut grass, picked up trash, or worked a vegetable garden at Julia Tutwiler State Prison for Women. This attempt to institute chain gangs for women was in part a response to lawsuits by male prisoners, who charged that male chain gains discriminated against men by virtue of their gender.[92] However, immediately after Jones's announcement, Governor Fob James, who obviously was pressured to prevent Alabama from acquiring the dubious distinction of being the only U.S. state to have equal- opportunity chain gangs, fired him.

Shortly after Alabama's embarrassing flirtation with the possibility of chain gangs for women, Sheriff Joe Arpaio of Maricopo County, Arizona—represented in the media as "the toughest sheriff in America"—held a press conference to announce that because he was "an equal opportunity incarcerator," he was establishing the country's first female chain gang.[93] When the plan was implemented, newspapers throughout the country carried a photograph of chained women cleaning Phoenix's streets. Even though this may have been a publicity stunt designed to bolster the fame of Sheriff Arpaio, the fact that this women's chain gang emerged against the backdrop of a generalized increase in the repression inflicted on women prisoners is certainly cause for alarm. Women's prisons throughout the country increasingly include sections known as security housing units. The regimes of solitary confinement and sensory deprivation in the security housing unit (SHU) in these sections within women's prisons are smaller versions of the rapidly proliferating super-maximum security prisons. Since the population of women in prison now consists of a majority of women of color, the historical resonances of slavery, colonization, and genocide should not be missed in these images of women in chains and shackles.

As the level of repression in women's prisons increases, and, paradoxically, as the influence of domestic prison regimes recedes, sexual abuse—which, like domestic violence, is yet another dimension of the privatized punishment of women—has become an institutionalized component of punishment behind prison walls. Although guard-on-prisoner sexual abuse is not sanctioned as such, the widespread leniency with which offending officers are treated suggests that for women, prison is a space in which the threat of sexualized violence that looms in the larger socie-

sexual abuse in prisons

ty is effectively sanctioned as a routine aspect of the landscape of punishment behind prison walls.

According to a 1996 Human Rights Watch report on the sexual abuse of women in U.S. prisons:

> Our findings indicate that being a woman prisoner in U.S. state prisons can be a terrifying experience. If you are sexually abused, you cannot escape from your abuser. Grievance or investigatory procedures, where they exist, are often ineffectual, and correctional employees continue to engage in abuse because they believe they will rarely be held accountable, administratively or criminally. Few people outside the prison walls know what is going on or care if they do know. Fewer still do anything to address the problem.[94]

The following excerpt from the summary of this report, entitled *All Too Familiar: Sexual Abuse of Women in U.S. State Prisons,* reveals the extent to which women's prison environments are violently sexualized, thus recapitulating the familiar violence that characterizes many women's private lives:

> We found that male correctional employees have vaginally, anally, and orally raped female prisoners and sexually assaulted and abused them. We found that in the course of committing such gross misconduct, male officers have not only used actual or threatened physical force, but have also used their near total authority to provide or deny goods and privileges to female prisoners to compel them to have sex or, in other cases, to reward them for hav-

ing done so. In other cases, male officers have violated their most basic professional duty and engaged in sexual contact with female prisoners absent the use of threat of force or any material exchange. In addition to engaging in sexual relations with prisoners, male officers have used mandatory pat-frisks or room searches to grope women's breasts, buttocks, and vaginal areas and to view them inappropriately while in a state of undress in the housing or bathroom areas. Male correctional officers and staff have also engaged in regular verbal degradation and harassment of female prisoners, thus contributing to a custodial environment in the state prisons for women that is often highly sexualized and excessively hostile.[95]

The violent sexualization of prison life within women's institutions raises a number of issues that may help us develop further our critique of the prison system. Ideologies of sexuality—and particularly the intersection of race and sexuality—have had a profound effect on the representations of and treatment received by women of color both within and outside prison. Of course, black and Latino men experience a perilous continuity in the way they are treated in school, where they are disciplined as potential criminals; in the streets, where they are subjected to racial profiling by the police; and in prison, where they are warehoused and deprived of virtually all of their rights. For women, the continuity of treatment from the free world to the universe of the prison is even more complicated, since they also confront forms of violence in prison that they have confronted in their homes and intimate relationships.

The criminalization of black and Latina women includes

persisting images of hypersexuality that serve to justify sexual assaults against them both in and outside of prison. Such images were vividly rendered in a *Nightline* television series filmed in November 1999 on location at California's Valley State Prison for Women. Many of the women interviewed by Ted Koppel complained that they received frequent and unnecessary pelvic examinations, including when they visited the doctor with such routine illnesses as colds. In an attempt to justify these examinations, the chief medical officer explained that women prisoners had rare opportunities for "male contact," and that they therefore welcomed these superfluous gynecological exams. Although this officer was eventually removed from his position as a result of these comments, his reassignment did little to alter the pervasive vulnerability of imprisoned women to sexual abuse.

Studies on female prisons throughout the world indicate that sexual abuse is an abiding, though unacknowledged, form of punishment to which women, who have the misfortune of being sent to prison, are subjected. This is one aspect of life in prison that women can expect to encounter, either directly or indirectly, regardless of the written policies that govern the institution. In June 1998, Radhika Coomaraswamy, the United Nations Special Rapporteur for Violence Against Women, visited federal and state prisons as well as Immigration and Naturalization detention facilities in New York, Connecticut, New Jersey, Minnesota, Georgia, and California. She was refused permission to visit women's prisons in Michigan, where serious allegations of sexual abuse were pending. In the aftermath of her visits, Coomaraswamy announced that "sexual misconduct by prison staff is widespread in American women's prisons."[96]

This clandestine institutionalization of sexual abuse vio-

UN rules

lates one of the guiding principles of the United Nations' Standard Minimum Rules for the Treatment of Prisoners, a UN instrument first adopted in 1955 and used as a guideline by many governments to achieve what is known as "good prison practice." However, the U.S. government has done little to publicize these rules and it is probably the case that most correctional personnel have never heard of these UN standards. According to the Standard Minimum Rules,

> Imprisonment and other measures which result in cutting off an offender from the outside world are afflictive by the very fact of taking from the person the right of self-determination by depriving him of his liberty. Therefore the prison system shall not, except as incidental to justifiable segregation or the maintenance of discipline, aggravate the suffering inherent in such a situation.[97]

Sexual abuse is surreptitiously incorporated into one of *the* the most habitual aspects of women's imprisonment, the *strip search* strip search. As activists and prisoners themselves have pointed out, the state itself is directly implicated in this routinization of sexual abuse, both in permitting such conditions that render women vulnerable to explicit sexual coercion carried out by guards and other prison staff and by incorporating into routine policy such practices as the strip search and body cavity search.

Australian lawyer/activist Amanda George has pointed out that

> [t]he acknowledgement that sexual assault does occur in institutions for people with intellectual disabilities, prisons, psychiatric hospitals, youth

training centres and police stations, usually centres around the criminal acts of rape and sexual assault by individuals employed in those institutions. These offences, though they are rarely reported, are clearly understood as being "crimes" for which the individual and not the state is responsible. At the same time as the state deplores "unlawful" sexual assaults by its employees, it actually uses sexual assault as a means of control.

In Victoria, prison and police officers are vested with the power and responsibility to do acts which, if done outside of work hours, would be crimes of sexual assault. If a person does not "consent" to being stripped naked by these officers, force can lawfully be used to do it . . . These legal strip searches are, in the author's view, sexual assaults within the definition of indecent assault in the *Crimes Act 1958 (Vic)* as amended in section 39.[98]

At a November 2001 conference on women in prison held by the Brisbane-based organization Sisters Inside, Amanda George described an action performed before a national gathering of correctional personnel working in women's prisons. Several women seized control of the stage and, some playing guards, others playing the roles of prisoners, dramatized a strip search. According to George, the gathering was so repulsed by this enactment of a practice that occurs routinely in women's prisons everywhere that many of the participants felt compelled to disassociate themselves from such practices, insisting that this was not what they did. Some of the guards, George said, simply cried upon watching representations of their own actions outside the prison context. What they must have realized is that "without the

uniform, without the power of the state, [the strip search] would be sexual assault."[99]

But why is an understanding of the pervasiveness of sexual abuse in women's prisons an important element of a radical analysis of the prison system, and especially of those forward-looking analyses that lead us in the direction of abolition? Because the call to abolish the prison as the dominant form of punishment cannot ignore the extent to which the institution of the prison has stockpiled ideas and practices that are hopefully approaching obsolescence in the larger society, but that retain all their ghastly vitality behind prison walls. The destructive combination of racism and misogyny, however much it has been challenged by social movements, scholarship, and art over the last three decades, retains all its awful consequences within women's prisons. The relatively uncontested presence of sexual abuse in women's prisons is one of many such examples. The increasing evidence of a U.S. prison industrial complex with global resonances leads us to think about the extent to which the many corporations that have acquired an investment in the expansion of the prison system are, like the state, directly implicated in an institution that perpetuates violence against women.

5

The Prison Industrial Complex

"For private business prison labor is like a pot of gold. No strikes. No union organizing. No health benefits, unemployment insurance, or workers' compensation to pay. No language barriers, as in foreign countries. New leviathan prisons are being built on thousands of eerie acres of factories inside the walls. Prisoners do data entry for Chevron, make telephone reservations for TWA, raise hogs, shovel manure, and make circuit boards, limousines, waterbeds, and lingerie for Victoria's Secret, all at a fraction of the cost of 'free labor.'"

—Linda Evans and Eve Goldberg[100]

The exploitation of prison labor by private corporations is one aspect among an array of relationships linking corporations, government, correctional communities, and media. These relationships constitute what we now call a prison industrial complex. The term "prison industrial complex" was introduced by activists and scholars to contest prevailing beliefs that increased levels of crime were the root cause of mounting prison populations. Instead, they argued, prison construction and the attendant drive to fill these new structures with human bodies have been driven by ideologies of racism and the pursuit of profit. Social historian Mike Davis first used the term in relation to California's penal system, which, he observed, already had begun in the 1990s to rival

agribusiness and land development as a major economic and political force.[101]

To understand the social meaning of the prison today within the context of a developing prison industrial complex means that punishment has to be conceptually severed from its seemingly indissoluble link with crime. How often do we encounter the phrase "crime and punishment"? To what extent has the perpetual repetition of the phrase "crime and punishment" in literature, as titles of television shows, both fictional and documentary, and in everyday conversation made it extremely difficult to think about punishment beyond this connection? How have these portrayals located the prison in a causal relation to crime as a natural, necessary, and permanent effect, thus inhibiting serious debates about the viability of the prison today?

The notion of a prison industrial complex insists on understandings of the punishment process that take into account economic and political structures and ideologies, rather than focusing myopically on individual criminal conduct and efforts to "curb crime." The fact, for example, that many corporations with global markets now rely on prisons as an important source of profit helps us to understand the rapidity with which prisons began to proliferate precisely at a time when official studies indicated that the crime rate was falling. The notion of a prison industrial complex also insists that the racialization of prison populations—and this is not only true of the United States, but of Europe, South America, and Australia as well—is not an incidental feature. Thus, critiques of the prison industrial complex undertaken by abolitionist activists and scholars are very much linked to critiques of the global persistence of racism. Antiracist and other social justice movements are incomplete with attention to the politics of imprisonment. At the 2001

United Nations World Conference Against Racism held in Durban, South Africa, a few individuals active in abolitionist campaigns in various countries attempted to bring this connection to the attention of the international community. They pointed out that the expanding system of prisons throughout the world both relies on and further promotes structures of racism even though its proponents may adamantly maintain that it is race-neutral.

Some critics of the prison system have employed the term "correctional industrial complex" and others "penal industrial complex." These and the term I have chosen to underscore, "prison industrial complex," all clearly resonate with the historical concept of a "military industrial complex," whose usage dates back to the presidency of Dwight Eisenhower. It may seem ironic that a Republican president was the first to underscore a growing and dangerous alliance between the military and corporate worlds, but it clearly seemed right to antiwar activists and scholars during the era of the Vietnam War. Today, some activists mistakenly argue that the prison industrial complex is moving into the space vacated by the military industrial complex. However, the so-called War on Terrorism initiated by the Bush administration in the aftermath of the 2002 attacks on the World Trade Center has made it very clear that the links between the military, corporations, and government are growing stronger, not weaker.

A more cogent way to define the relationship between the military industrial complex and the prison industrial complex would be to call it symbiotic. These two complexes mutually support and promote each other and, in fact, often share technologies. During the early nineties, when defense production was temporarily on the decline, this connection between the military industry and the criminal jus-

tice/punishment industry was acknowledged in a 1994 *Wall Street Journal* article entitled "Making Crime Pay: The Cold War of the '90s":

> Parts of the defense establishment are cashing in, too, sensing a logical new line of business to help them offset military cutbacks. Westinghouse Electric Corp., Minnesota Mining and Manufacturing Co, GDE Systems (a division of the old General Dynamics) and Alliant Techsystems Inc., for instance, are pushing crime fighting equipment and have created special divisions to retool their defense technology for America's streets.[102]

The article describes a conference sponsored by the National Institute of Justice, the research arm of the Justice Department, entitled "Law Enforcement Technology in the 21st Century." The secretary of defense was a major presenter at this conference, which explored topics such as, "The role of the defense industry, particularly for dual use and conversion."

> Hot topics: defense-industry technology that could lower the level of violence involved in crime fighting. Sandia National Laboratories, for instance, is experimenting with a dense foam that can be sprayed at suspects, temporarily blinding and deafening them under breathable bubbles. Stinger Corporation is working on "smart guns," which will fire only for the owner, and retractable spiked barrier strips to unfurl in front of fleeing vehicles. Westinghouse is promoting the "smart car," in which minicomputers could be linked up with big

mainframes at the police department, allowing for speedy booking of prisoners, as well as quick exchanges of information . . .[103]

But an analysis of the relationship between the military and prison industrial complex is not only concerned with the transference of technologies from the military to the law enforcement industry. What may be even more important to our discussion is the extent to which both share important structural features. Both systems generate huge profits from processes of social destruction. Precisely that which is advantageous to those corporations, elected officials, and government agents who have obvious stakes in the expansion of these systems begets grief and devastation for poor and racially dominated communities in the United States and throughout the world. The transformation of imprisoned bodies—and they are in their majority bodies of color—into sources of profit who consume and also often produce all kinds of commodities, devours public funds, which might otherwise be available for social programs such as education, housing, childcare, recreation, and drug programs.

Punishment no longer constitutes a marginal area of the larger economy. Corporations producing all kinds of goods—from buildings to electronic devices and hygiene products—and providing all kinds of services—from meals to therapy and healthcare—are now directly involved in the punishment business. That is to say, companies that one would assume are far removed from the work of state punishment have developed major stakes in the perpetuation of a prison system whose historical obsolescence is therefore that much more difficult to recognize. It was during the decade of the 1980s that corporate ties to the punishment system became

more extensive and entrenched than ever before. But throughout the history of the U.S. prison system, prisoners have always constituted a potential source of profit. For example, they have served as valuable subjects in medical research, thus positioning the prison as a major link between universities and corporations.

During the post–World War II period, for example, medical experimentation on captive populations helped to hasten the development of the pharmaceutical industry. According to Allen Hornblum,

> [T]he number of American medical research programs that relied on prisoners as subjects rapidly expanded as zealous doctors and researchers, grant-making universities, and a burgeoning pharmaceutical industry raced for greater market share. Society's marginal people were, as they had always been, the grist for the medical-pharmaceutical mill, and prison inmates in particular would become the raw materials for postwar profit-making and academic advancement.[104]

Hornblum's book, *Acres of Skin: Human Experiments at Holmesburg Prison*, highlights the career of research dermatologist Albert Kligman, who was a professor at the University of Pennsylvania. Kligman, the "Father of Retin-A,"[105] conducted hundreds of experiments on the men housed in Holmesburg Prison and, in the process, trained many researchers to use what were later recognized as unethical research methods.

> When Dr. Kligman entered the aging prison he was awed by the potential it held for his research. In

1966, he recalled in a newspaper interview: "All I saw before me were acres of skin. It was like a farmer seeing a fertile field for the first time." The hundreds of inmates walking aimlessly before him represented a unique opportunity for unlimited and undisturbed medical research. He described it in this interview as "an anthropoid colony, mainly healthy" under perfect control conditions.[106]

By the time the experimentation program was shut down in 1974 and new federal regulations prohibited the use of prisoners as subjects for academic and corporate research, numerous cosmetics and skin creams had already been tested. Some of them had caused great harm to these subjects and could not be marketed in their original form. Johnson and Johnson, Ortho Pharmaceutical, and Dow Chemical are only a few of the corporations that reaped great material benefits from these experiments.

The potential impact of corporate involvement in punishment could have been glimpsed in the Kligman experiments at Holmesburg Prison as early as the 1950s and 1960s. However, it was not until the 1980s and the increasing globalization of capitalism that the massive surge of capital into the punishment economy began. The deindustrialization processes that resulted in plant shutdowns throughout the country created a huge pool of vulnerable human beings, a pool of people for whom no further jobs were available. This also brought more people into contact with social services, such as AFDC (Aid to Families with Dependent Children) and other welfare agencies. It is not accidental that "welfare, as we have known it"—to use former President Clinton's words—came under severe attack and was eventually disestablished. This was known as "welfare reform." At the same

time, we experienced the privatization and corporatization of services that were previously run by government. The most obvious example of this privatization process was the transformation of government-run hospitals and health services into a gigantic complex of what are euphemistically called health maintenance organizations. In this sense we might also speak of a "medical industrial complex."[107] In fact, there is a connection between one of the first private hospital companies, Hospital Corporation of America—known today as HCA—and Corrections Corporation of America (CCA). Board members of HCA, which today has two hundred hospitals and seventy outpatient surgery centers in twenty-four states, England, and Switzerland helped to start Correctional Corporations of America in 1983.

In the context of an economy that was driven by an unprecedented pursuit of profit, no matter what the human cost, and the concomitant dismantling of the welfare state, poor people's abilities to survive became increasingly constrained by the looming presence of the prison. The massive prison-building project that began in the 1980s created the means of concentrating and managing what the capitalist system had implicitly declared to be a human surplus. In the meantime, elected officials and the dominant media justified the new draconian sentencing practices, sending more and more people to prison in the frenzied drive to build more and more prisons by arguing that this was the only way to make our communities safe from murderers, rapists, and robbers.

> The media, especially television . . . have a vested interest in perpetuating the notion that crime is out of control. With new competition from cable networks and 24-hour news channels, TV news and programs about crime . . . have proliferated madly.

According to the Center for Media and Public Affairs, crime coverage was the number-one topic on the nightly news over the past decade. From 1990 to 1998, homicide rates dropped by half nationwide, but homicide stories on the three major networks rose almost fourfold.[108]

During the same period when crime rates were declining, prison populations soared. According to a recent report by the U.S. Department of Justice, at the end of the year 2001, there were 2,100,146 people incarcerated in the United States.[109] The terms and numbers as they appear in this government report require some preliminary discussion. I hesitate to make unmediated use of such statistical evidence because it can discourage the very critical thinking that ought to be elicited by an understanding of the prison industrial complex. It is precisely the abstraction of numbers that plays such a central role in criminalizing those who experience the misfortune of imprisonment. There are many different kinds of men and women in the prisons, jails, and INS and military detention centers, whose lives are erased by the Bureau of Justice Statistics figures. The numbers recognize no distinction between the woman who is imprisoned on drug conspiracy and the man who is in prison for killing his wife, a man who might actually end up spending less time behind bars than the woman.

With this observation in mind, the statistical breakdown is as follows: There were 1,324,465 people in "federal and state prisons," 15,852 in "territorial prisons," 631,240 in "local jails," 8,761 in "Immigration and Naturalization Service detention facilities," 2,436 in "military facilities," 1,912 in "jails in Indian country," and 108,965 in "juvenile facilities." In the ten years between 1990 and 2000, 351 new places of

'90-'00 — 81% increase in state facilities

confinement were opened by states and more than 528,000 beds were added, amounting to 1,320 state facilities, representing an eighty-one percent increase. Moreover, there are currently 84 federal facilities and 264 private facilities.[10]

The government reports, from which these figures are taken, emphasize the extent to which incarceration rates are slowing down. The Bureau of Justice Statistics report entitled "Prisoners in 2001" introduces the study by indicating that "the Nation's prison population grew 1.1%, which was less than the average annual growth of 3.8% since yearend 1995. During 2001 the prison population rose at the lowest rate since 1972 and had the smallest absolute increase since 1979."[11] However small the increase, these numbers themselves would defy the imagination were they not so neatly classified and rationally organized. To place these figures in historical perspective, try to imagine how people in the eighteenth and nineteenth centuries—and indeed for most of the twentieth century—who welcomed the new, and then quite extraordinary, system of punishment called the prison might have responded had they known that such a colossal number of lives would be eventually claimed permanently by this institution. I have already shared my own memories of a time three decades ago when the prison population was comprised of a tenth of the present numbers.

1980— only a tenth of Today's prison pop

The prison industrial complex is fueled by privatization patterns that, it will be recalled, have also drastically transformed health care, education, and other areas of our lives. Moreover, the prison privatization trends—both the increasing presence of corporations in the prison economy and the establishment of private prisons—are reminiscent of the historical efforts to create a profitable punishment industry based on the new supply of "free" black male laborers in the

aftermath of the Civil War. Steven Donziger, drawing from the work of Norwegian criminologist Nils Christie, argues:

> [C]ompanies that service the criminal justice system need sufficient quantities of raw materials to guarantee long-term growth . . . In the criminal justice field, *the raw material is prisoners*, and industry will do what is necessary to guarantee a steady supply. For the supply of prisoners to grow, criminal justice policies must ensure a sufficient number of incarcerated Americans regardless of whether crime is rising or the incarceration is necessary.[112]

In the post–Civil War era, emancipated black men and women comprised an enormous reservoir of labor at a time when planters—and industrialists—could no longer rely on slavery, as they had done in the past. This labor became increasingly available for use by private agents precisely through the convict lease system, discussed earlier, and related systems such as debt peonage. Recall that in the aftermath of slavery, the penal population drastically shifted, so that in the South it rapidly became disproportionately black. This transition set the historical stage for the easy acceptance of disproportionately black prison populations today. According to 2002 Bureau of Justice Statistics, African-Americans as a whole now represent the majority of county, state, and federal prisoners, with a total of 803,400 black inmates—118, 600 more than the total number of white inmates. If we include Latinos, we must add another 283,000 bodies of color.[113]

As the rate of increase in the incarceration of black prisoners continues to rise, the racial composition of the incarcerated population is approaching the proportion of black

prisoners to white during the era of the southern convict lease and county chain gang systems. Whether this human raw material is used for purposes of labor or for the consumption of commodities provided by a rising number of corporations directly implicated in the prison industrial complex, it is clear that black bodies are considered dispensable within the "free world" but as a major source of profit in the prison world.

The privatization characteristic of convict leasing has its contemporary parallels, as companies such as CCA and Wackenhut literally run prisons for profit. At the beginning of the twenty-first century, the numerous private prison companies operating in the United States own and operate facilities that hold 91,828 federal and state prisoners.[114] Texas and Oklahoma can claim the largest number of people in private prisons. But New Mexico imprisons forty-four percent of its prison population in private facilities, and states such as Montana, Alaska, and Wyoming turned over more than twenty-five percent of their prison population to private companies.[115] In arrangements reminiscent of the convict lease system, federal, state, and county governments pay private companies a fee for each inmate, which means that private companies have a stake in retaining prisoners as long as possible, and in keeping their facilities filled.

In the state of Texas, there are thirty-four government-owned, privately run jails in which approximately 5,500 out-of-state prisoners are incarcerated. These facilities generate about eighty million dollars annually for Texas.[116] One dramatic example involves Capital Corrections Resources, Inc., which operates the Brazoria Detention Center, a government-owned facility located forty miles outside of Houston, Texas. Brazoria came to public attention in August 1997 when a videotape broadcast on national television showed prisoners

there being bitten by police dogs and viciously kicked in the groin and stepped on by guards. The inmates, forced to crawl on the floor, also were being shocked with stun guns, while guards—who referred to one black prisoner as "boy"—shouted, "Crawl faster!"[117] In the aftermath of the release of this tape, the state of Missouri withdrew the 415 prisoners it housed in the Brazoria Detention Center. Although few references were made in the accompanying news reports to the indisputably racialized character of the guards' outrageous behavior, in the section of the Brazoria videotape that was shown on national television, black male prisoners were seen to be the primary targets of the guards' attacks.

The thirty-two-minute Brazoria tape, represented by the jail authorities as a training tape—allegedly showing corrections officers "what *not* to do"—was made in September 1996, after a guard allegedly smelled marijuana in the jail. Important evidence of the abuse that takes place behind the walls and gates of private prisons, it came to light in connection with a lawsuit filed by one of the prisoners who was bitten by a dog; he was suing Brazoria County for a hundred thousand dollars in damage. The Brazoria jailors' actions—which, according to prisoners there, were far worse than depicted on the tape—are indicative not only of the ways in which many prisoners throughout the country are treated, but of generalized attitudes toward people locked up in jails and prisons.

According to an Associated Press news story, the Missouri inmates, once they had been transferred back to their home state from Brazoria, told the *Kansas City Star*:

> [G]uards at the Brazoria County Detention Center used cattle prods and other forms of intimidation to win respect and force prisoners to say, "I love Texas." "What you saw on tape wasn't a fraction of

what happened that day," said inmate Louis Watkins, referring to the videotaped cellblock raid of September 18, 1996. "I've never seen anything like that in the movies."[118]

In 2000 there were twenty-six for-profit prison corporations in the United States that operated approximately 150 facilities in twenty-eight states.[119] The largest of these companies, CCA and Wackenhut, control 76.4 percent of the private prison market globally. CCA is headquartered in Nashville, Tennessee, and until 2001 its largest shareholder was the multinational headquartered in Paris, Sodexho Alliance, which, through its U.S. subsidiary, Sodexho Marriott, provides catering services at nine hundred U.S. colleges and universities. The Prison Moratorium Project, an organization promoting youth activism, led a protest campaign against Sodexho Marriott on campuses throughout the country. Among the campuses that dropped Sodexho were SUNY Albany, Goucher College, and James Madison University. Students had staged sit-ins and organized rallies on more than fifty campuses before Sodexho divested its holdings in CCA in fall 2001.[120]

Though private prisons represent a fairly small proportion of prisons in the United States, the privatization model is quickly becoming the primary mode of organizing punishment in many other countries.[121] These companies have tried to take advantage of the expanding population of women prisoners, both in the United States and globally. In 1996, the first private women's prison was established by CCA in Melbourne, Australia. The government of Victoria "adopted the U.S. model of privatization in which financing, design, construction, and ownership of the prison are awarded to one contractor and the government pays them back for

*the looming power of the private prison industry

construction over twenty years. This means that it is virtually impossible to remove the contractor because that contractor owns the prison."[122]

As a direct consequence of the campaign organized by prison activist groups in Melbourne, Victoria withdrew the contract from CCA in 2001. However, a significant portion of Australia's prison system remains privatized. In the fall of 2002, the government of Queensland renewed Wackenhut's contract to run a 710-bed prison in Brisbane. The value of the five-year contract is $66.5 million. In addition to the facility in Brisbane, Wackenhut manages eleven other prisons in Australia and New Zealand and furnishes health care services in eleven public prisons in the state of Victoria.[123] In the press release announcing this contract renewal, Wackenhut describes its global business activities as follows:

> WCC, a world leader in the privatized corrections industry, has contracts/awards to manage 60 correctional/detention facilities in North America, Europe, Australia, South Africa and New Zealand with a total of approximately 43,000 beds. WCC also provides prisoner transportation services, electronic monitoring for home detainees, correctional health care and mental health services. WCC offers government agencies a turnkey approach to the development of new correctional and mental health institutions that includes design, construction, financing, and operations.[124]

But to understand the reach of the prison industrial complex, it is not enough to evoke the looming power of the private prison business. By definition, those companies court the state within and outside the United States for the pur-

pose of obtaining prison contracts, bringing punishment and profit together in a menacing embrace. Still, this is only the most visible dimension of the prison industrial complex, and it should not lead us to ignore the more comprehensive corporatization that is a feature of contemporary punishment. As compared to earlier historical eras, the prison economy is no longer a small, identifiable, and containable set of markets. Many corporations, whose names are highly recognizable by "free world" consumers, have discovered new possibilities for expansion by selling their products to correctional facilities.

many corporations sell to prisons

> In the 1990s, the variety of corporations making money from prisons is truly dizzying, ranging from Dial Soap to Famous Amos cookies, from AT&T to health-care providers . . . In 1995 Dial Soap sold $100,000 worth of its product to the New York City jail system alone . . . When VitaPro Foods of Montreal, Canada, contracted to supply inmates in the state of Texas with its soy-based meat substitute, the contract was worth $34 million a year.[125]

Among the many businesses that advertise in the yellow pages on the corrections.com Web site are Archer Daniel Midlands, Nestle Food Service, Ace Hardware, Polaroid, Hewlett-Packard, RJ Reynolds, and the communications companies Sprint, AT&T, Verizon, and Ameritech. One conclusion to be drawn here is that even if private prison companies were prohibited—an unlikely prospect, indeed—the prison industrial complex and its many strategies for profit would remain relatively intact. Private prisons are direct sources of profit for the companies that run them, but public prisons have become so thoroughly saturated with the

profit-producing products and services of private corporations that the distinction is not as meaningful as one might suspect. Campaigns against privatization that represent public prisons as an adequate alternative to private prisons can be misleading. It is true that a major reason for the profitability of private prisons consists in the nonunion labor they employ, and this important distinction should be highlighted. Nevertheless, public prisons are now equally tied to the corporate economy and constitute an ever-growing source of capitalist profit.

Extensive corporate investment in prisons has significantly raised the stakes for antiprison work. It means that serious antiprison activists must be willing to look much further in their analyses and organizing strategies than the actual institution of the prison. Prison reform rhetoric, which has always undergirded dominant critiques of the prison system, will not work in this new situation. If reform approaches have tended to bolster the permanence of the prison in the past, they certainly will not suffice to challenge the economic and political relationships that sustain the prison today. This means that in the era of the prison industrial complex, activists must pose hard questions about the relationship between global capitalism and the spread of U.S.-style prisons throughout the world.

The global prison economy is indisputably dominated by the United States. This economy not only consists of the products, services, and ideas that are directly marketed to other governments, but it also exercises an enormous influence over the development of the style of state punishment throughout the world. One dramatic example can be seen in the opposition to Turkey's attempts to transform its prisons. In October 2000, prisoners in Turkey, many of whom are associated with left political movements, began a "death

fast" as a way of dramatizing their opposition to the Turkish government's decision to introduce "F-Type," or U.S.-style, prisons. Compared to the traditional dormitory-style facilities, these new prisons consist of one- to three-person cells, which are opposed by the prisoners because of the regimes of isolation they facilitate and because mistreatment and torture are far more likely in isolation. In December 2000, thirty prisoners were killed in clashes with security forces in twenty prisons.[126] As of September 2002, more than fifty prisoners have died of hunger, including two women, Gulnihal Yilmaz and Birsen Hosver, who were among the most recent prisoners to succumb to the death fast.

"F-Type" prisons in Turkey were inspired by the recent emergence of the super-maximum security—or supermax—prison in the United States, which presumes to control otherwise unmanageable prisoners by holding them in permanent solitary confinement and by subjecting them to varying degrees of sensory deprivation. In its *2002 World Report*, Human Rights Watch paid particular attention to the concerns raised by

> the spread of ultra-modern "super-maximum" security prisons. Originally prevalent in the United States . . . the supermax model was increasingly followed in other countries. Prisoners confined in such facilities spent an average of twenty-three hours a day in their cells, enduring extreme social isolation, enforced idleness, and extraordinarily limited recreational and educational opportunities. While prison authorities defended the use of super-maximum security facilities by asserting that they held only the most dangerous, disruptive, or escape-prone inmates, few safeguards existed to prevent

other prisoners from being arbitrarily or discriminatorily transferred to such facilities. In Australia, the inspector of custodial services found that some prisoners were being held indefinitely in special high security units without knowing why or when their isolation would end.[127]

Among the many countries that have recently constructed super-maximum security prisons is South Africa. Construction was completed on the supermax prison in Kokstad, KwaZulu-Natal in August 2000, but it was not officially opened until May 2002. Ironically, the reason given for the delay was the competition for water between the prison and a new low-cost housing development.[128] I am highlighting South Africa's embrace of the supermax because of the apparent ease with which this most repressive version of the U.S. prison has established itself in a country that has just recently initiated the project of building a democratic, nonracist, and nonsexist society. South Africa was the first country in the world to create constitutional assurances for gay rights, and it immediately abolished the death penalty after the dismantling of apartheid. Nevertheless, following the example of the United States, the South African prison system is expanding and becoming more oppressive. The U.S. private prison company Wackenhut has secured several contracts with the South African government and by constructing private prisons further legitimizes the trend toward privatization (which affects the availability of basic services from utilities to education) in the economy as a whole.

South Africa's participation in the prison industrial complex constitutes a major impediment to the creation of a democratic society. In the United States, we have already felt the insidious and socially damaging effects of prison

expansion. The dominant social expectation is that young black, Latino, Native American, and Southeast Asian men—and increasingly women as well—will move naturally from the free world into prison, where, it is assumed, they belong. Despite the important gains of antiracist social movements over the last half century, racism hides from view within institutional structures, and its most reliable refuge is the prison system.

The racist arrests of vast numbers of immigrants from Middle Eastern countries in the aftermath of the attacks on September 11, 2001, and the subsequent withholding of information about the names of numbers of people held in INS detention centers, some of which are owned and operated by private corporations, do not augur a democratic future. The uncontested detention of increasing numbers of undocumented immigrants from the global South has been aided considerably by the structures and ideologies associated with the prison industrial complex. We can hardly move in the direction of justice and equality in the twenty-first century if we are unwilling to recognize the enormous role played by this system in extending the power of racism and xenophobia.

Radical opposition to the global prison industrial complex sees the antiprison movement as a vital means of expanding the terrain on which the quest for democracy will unfold. This movement is thus antiracist, anticapitalist, antisexist, and antihomophobic. It calls for the abolition of the prison as the dominant mode of punishment but at the same time recognizes the need for genuine solidarity with the millions of men, women, and children who are behind bars. A major challenge of this movement is to do the work that will create more humane, habitable environments for people in prison without bolstering the permanence of the prison system. How, then, do we accomplish this balancing

act of passionately attending to the needs of prisoners—calling for less violent conditions, an end to state sexual assault, improved physical and mental health care, greater access to drug programs, better educational work opportunities, unionization of prison labor, more connections with families and communities, shorter or alternative sentencing—and at the same time call for alternatives to sentencing altogether, no more prison construction, and abolitionist strategies that question the place of the prison in our future?

6

Abolitionist Alternatives

"Forget about reform; it's time to talk about abolishing jails and prisons in American society . . . Still—abolition? Where do you put the prisoners? The 'criminals'? What's the alternative? First, having no alternative at all would create less crime than the present criminal training centers do. Second, the only full alternative is building the kind of society that does not need prisons: A decent redistribution of power and income so as to put out the hidden fire of burning envy that now flames up in crimes of property—both burglary by the poor and embezzlement by the affluent. And a decent sense of community that can support, reintegrate and truly rehabilitate those who suddenly become filled with fury or despair, and that can face them not as objects—'criminals'—but as people who have committed illegal acts, as have almost all of us."

—Arthur Waskow, Institute for Policy Studies[129]

If jails and prisons are to be abolished, then what will replace them? This is the puzzling question that often interrupts further consideration of the prospects for abolition. Why should it be so difficult to imagine alternatives to our current system of incarceration? There are a number of reasons why we tend to balk at the idea that it may be possible to eventually create an entirely different—and perhaps more egalitarian—system of justice. First of all, we think of the

current system, with its exaggerated dependence on imprisonment, as an unconditional standard and thus have great difficulty envisioning any other way of dealing with the more than two million people who are currently being held in the country's jails, prisons, youth facilities, and immigration detention centers. Ironically, even the anti–death penalty campaign tends to rely on the assumption that life imprisonment is the most rational alternative to capital punishment. As important as it may be to abolish the death penalty, we should be conscious of the way the contemporary campaign against capital punishment has a propensity to recapitulate the very historical patterns that led to the emergence of the prison as the dominant form of punishment. The death penalty has coexisted with the prison, though imprisonment was supposed to serve as an alternative to corporal and capital punishment. This is a major dichotomy. A critical engagement with this dichotomy would involve taking seriously the possibility of linking the goal of death penalty abolitionism with strategies for prison abolition.

It is true that if we focus myopically on the existing system—and perhaps this is the problem that leads to the assumption that imprisonment is the only alternative to death—it is very hard to imagine a structurally similar system capable of handling such a vast population of lawbreakers. If, however, we shift our attention from the prison, perceived as an isolated institution, to the set of relationships that comprise the prison industrial complex, it may be easier to think about alternatives. In other words, a more complicated framework may yield more options than if we simply attempt to discover a single substitute for the prison system. The first step, then, would be to let go of the desire to discover one single alternative system of punishment that would occupy the same footprint as the prison system.

Since the 1980s, the prison system has become increasingly ensconced in the economic, political and ideological life of the United States and the transnational trafficking in U.S. commodities, culture, and ideas. Thus, the prison industrial complex is much more than the sum of all the jails and prisons in this country. It is a set of symbiotic relationships among correctional communities, transnational corporations, media conglomerates, guards' unions, and legislative and court agendas. If it is true that the contemporary meaning of punishment is fashioned through these relationships, then the most effective abolitionist strategies will contest these relationships and propose alternatives that pull them apart. What, then, would it mean to imagine a system in which punishment is not allowed to become the source of corporate profit? How can we imagine a society in which race and class are not primary determinants of punishment? Or one in which punishment itself is no longer the central concern in the making of justice?

An abolitionist approach that seeks to answer questions such as these would require us to imagine a constellation of alternative strategies and institutions, with the ultimate aim of removing the prison from the social and ideological landscapes of our society. In other words, we would not be looking for prisonlike substitutes for the prison, such as house arrest safeguarded by electronic surveillance bracelets. Rather, positing decarceration as our overarching strategy, we would try to envision a continuum of alternatives to imprisonment—demilitarization of schools, revitalization of education at all levels, a health system that provides free physical and mental care to all, and a justice system based on reparation and reconciliation rather than retribution and vengeance.

The creation of new institutions that lay claim to the

space now occupied by the prison can eventually start to crowd out the prison so that it would inhabit increasingly smaller areas of our social and psychic landscape. Schools can therefore be seen as the most powerful alternative to jails and prisons. Unless the current structures of violence are eliminated from schools in impoverished communities of color—including the presence of armed security guards and police—and unless schools become places that encourage the joy of learning, these schools will remain the major conduits to prisons. The alternative would be to transform schools into vehicles for decarceration. Within the health care system, it is important to emphasize the current scarcity of institutions available to poor people who suffer severe mental and emotional illnesses. There are currently more people with mental and emotional disorders in jails and prisons than in mental institutions. This call for new facilities designed to assist poor people should not be taken as an appeal to reinstitute the old system of mental institutions, which were—and in many cases still are—as repressive as the prisons. It is simply to suggest that the racial and class disparities in care available to the affluent and the deprived need to be eradicated, thus creating another vehicle for decarceration.

To reiterate, rather than try to imagine one single alternative to the existing system of incarceration, we might envision an array of alternatives that will require radical transformations of many aspects of our society. Alternatives that fail to address racism, male dominance, homophobia, class bias, and other structures of domination will not, in the final analysis, lead to decarceration and will not advance the goal of abolition.

It is within this context that it makes sense to consider the decriminalization of drug use as a significant component of a larger strategy to simultaneously oppose structures of

racism within the criminal justice system and further the abolitionist agenda of decarceration. Thus, with respect to the project of challenging the role played by the so-called War on Drugs in bringing huge numbers of people of color into the prison system, proposals to decriminalize drug use should be linked to the development of a constellation of free, community-based programs accessible to all people who wish to tackle their drug problems. This is not to suggest that all people who use drugs—or that only people who use illicit drugs—need such help. However, anyone, regardless of economic status, who wishes to conquer drug addiction should be able to enter treatment programs.

Such institutions are, indeed, available to affluent communities. The most well known program is the Betty Ford Center, which, according to its Web site, "accepts patients dependent on alcohol and other mood altering chemicals. Treatment services are open to all men and women eighteen years of age and older regardless of race, creed, sex, national origin, religion or sources of payment for care."[130] However, the cost for the first six days is $1,175 per day, and after that $525 per day.[131] If a person requires thirty days of treatment, the cost would amount to $19,000, almost twice the annual salary of a person working a minimum-wage job.

Poor people deserve to have access to effective, voluntary drug treatment programs. Like the Betty Ford program, their operation should not be under the auspices of the criminal justice system. As at the Ford Center, family members also should be permitted to participate. But unlike the Betty Ford program, they should be free of charge. For such programs to count as "abolitionist alternatives," they would not be linked—unlike existing programs, to which individuals are "sentenced"—to imprisonment as a last resort.

The campaign to decriminalize drug use—from marijua-

na to heroin—is international in scope and has led countries such as the Netherlands to revise their laws, legalizing personal use of such drugs as marijuana and hashish. The Netherlands also has a history of legalized sex work, another area in which there has been extensive campaigning for decriminalization. In the cases of drugs and sex work, decriminalization would simply require repeal of all those laws that penalize individuals who use drugs and who work in the sex industry. The decriminalization of alcohol use serves as a historical example. In both these cases, decriminalization would advance the abolitionist strategy of decarceration—that is, the consistent reduction in the numbers of people who are sent to prison—with the ultimate aim of dismantling the prison system as the dominant mode of punishment. A further challenge for abolitionists is to identify other behaviors that might be appropriately decriminalized as preliminary steps toward abolition.

One obvious and very urgent aspect of the work of decriminalization is associated with the defense of immigrants' rights. The growing numbers of immigrants—especially since the attacks on September 11, 2001—who are incarcerated in immigrant detention centers, as well as in jails and prisons, can be halted by dismantling the processes that punish people for their failure to enter this country without documents. Current campaigns that call for the decriminalization of undocumented immigrants are making important contributions to the overall struggle against the prison industrial complex and are challenging the expansive reach of racism and male dominance. When women from countries in the southern region are imprisoned because they have entered this country to escape sexual violence, instead of being granted refugee status, this reinforces the generalized tendency to punish people who are persecuted in

their intimate lives as a direct consequence of pandemics of violence that continue to be legitimized by ideological and legal structures.

Within the United States, the "battered women's syndrome" legal defense reflects an attempt to argue that a woman who kills an abusive spouse should not be convicted of murder. This defense has been abundantly criticized, both by detractors and proponents of feminism; the former do not want to recognize the pervasiveness and dangers of intimate violence against women and the latter challenge the idea that the legitimacy of this defense resides in the assertion that those who kill their batterers are not responsible for their actions. The point feminist movements attempt to make—regardless of their specific positions on battered women's syndrome—is that violence against women is a pervasive and complicated social problem that cannot be solved by imprisoning women who fight back against their abusers. Thus, a vast range of alternative strategies of minimizing violence against women—within intimate relationships and within relationships to the state—should be the focus of our concern.

The alternatives toward which I have gestured thus far—and this is only a small selection of examples, which can also include job and living wage programs, alternatives to the disestablished welfare program, community-based recreation, and many more—are associated both directly and indirectly with the existing system of criminal justice. But, however mediated their relation might be to the current system of jails and prisons, these alternatives are attempting to reverse the impact of the prison industrial complex on our world. As they contest racism and other networks of social domination, their implementation will certainly advance the abolitionist agenda of decarceration.

Creating agendas of decarceration and broadly casting the net of alternatives helps us to do the ideological work of pulling apart the conceptual link between crime and punishment. This more nuanced understanding of the social role of the punishment system requires us to give up our usual way of thinking about punishment as an inevitable consequence of crime. We would recognize that "punishment" does not follow from "crime" in the neat and logical sequence offered by discourses that insist on the justice of imprisonment, but rather punishment—primarily through imprisonment (and sometimes death)—is linked to the agendas of politicians, the profit drive of corporations, and media representations of crime. Imprisonment is associated with the racialization of those most likely to be punished. It is associated with their class and, as we have seen, gender structures the punishment system as well. If we insist that abolitionist alternatives trouble these relationships, that they strive to disarticulate crime and punishment, race and punishment, class and punishment, and gender and punishment, then our focus must not rest only on the prison system as an isolated institution but must also be directed at all the social relations that support the permanence of the prison.

An attempt to create a new conceptual terrain for imagining alternatives to imprisonment involves the ideological work of questioning why "criminals" have been constituted as a class and, indeed, a class of human beings undeserving of the civil and human rights accorded to others. Radical criminologists have long pointed out that the category "lawbreakers" is far greater than the category of individuals who are deemed criminals since, many point out, almost all of us have broken the law at one time or another. Even President Bill Clinton admitted that he had smoked marijuana at one time, insisting, though, that he did not inhale. However,

acknowledged disparities in the intensity of police surveillance—as indicated by the present-day currency of the term "racial profiling" which ought to cover far more territory than "driving while black or brown"—account in part for racial and class-based disparities in arrest and imprisonment rates. Thus, if we are willing to take seriously the consequences of a racist and class-biased justice system, we will reach the conclusion that enormous numbers of people are in prison simply because they are, for example, black, Chicano, Vietnamese, Native American or poor, regardless of their ethnic background. They are sent to prison, not so much because of the crimes they may have indeed committed, but largely because their communities have been criminalized. Thus, programs for decriminalization will not only have to address specific activities that have been criminalized—such as drug use and sex work—but also criminalized populations and communities.

It is against the backdrop of these more broadly conceived abolitionist alternatives that it makes sense to take up the question of radical transformations within the existing justice system. Thus, aside from minimizing, through various strategies, the kinds of behaviors that will bring people into contact with the police and justice systems, there is the question of how to treat those who assault the rights and bodies of others. Many organizations and individuals both in the United States and other countries offer alternative modes of making justice. In limited instances, some governments have attempted to implement alternatives that range from conflict resolution to restorative or reparative justice. Such scholars as Herman Bianchi have suggested that crime needs to be defined in terms of tort and, instead of criminal law, should be reparative law. In his words, "[The lawbreaker] is thus no longer an evil-minded man or woman, but simply a debtor, a

liable person whose human duty is to take responsibility for his or her acts, and to assume the duty of repair."[132]

There is a growing body of literature on reshaping systems of justice around strategies of reparation, rather than retribution, as well as a growing body of experiential evidence of the advantages of these approaches to justice and of the democratic possibilities they promise. Instead of rehearsing the numerous debates that have emerged over the last decades—including the most persistent question, "What will happen to the murderers and rapists?"—I will conclude with a story of one of the most dramatic successes of these experiments in reconciliation. I refer to the case of Amy Biehl, the white Fulbright scholar from Newport Beach, California, who was killed by young South African men in Guguletu, a black township in Capetown, South Africa.

In 1993, when South Africa was on the cusp of its transition, Amy Biehl was devoting a significant amount of her time as a foreign student to the work of rebuilding South Africa. Nelson Mandela had been freed in 1990, but had not yet been elected president. On August 25, Biehl was driving several black friends to their home in Guguletu when a crowd shouting antiwhite slogans confronted her, and some of them stoned and stabbed her to death. Four of the men participating in the attack were convicted of her murder and sentenced to eighteen years in prison. In 1997, Linda and Peter Biehl—Amy's mother and father—decided to support the amnesty petition the men presented to the Truth and Reconciliation Commission. The four apologized to the Biehls and were released in July 1998. Two of them—Easy Nofemela and Ntobeko Peni—later met with the Biehls, who, despite much pressure to the contrary, agreed to see them.[133] According to Nofemela, he wanted to say more about his own sorrow for killing their daughter than what

had been possible during Truth and Reconciliation hearings. "I know you lost a person you love," he says he told them during that meeting. "I want you to forgive me and take me as your child."[134]

The Biehls, who had established the Amy Biehl Foundation in the aftermath of their daughter's death, asked Nofemela and Peni to work at the Guguletu branch of the foundation. Nofemela became an instructor in an after-school sports program and Peni an administrator. In June 2002, they accompanied Linda Biehl to New York, where they all spoke before the American Family Therapy Academy on reconciliation and restorative justice. In a *Boston Globe* interview, Linda Biehl, when asked how she now feels about the men who killed her daughter, said, "I have a lot of love for them." After Peter Biehl died in 2002, she bought two plots of land for them in memory of her husband so that Nofemela and Peni can build their own homes.[135] A few days after the September 11 attacks, the Biehls had been asked to speak at a synagogue in their community. According to Peter Biehl, "We tried to explain that sometimes it pays to shut up and listen to what other people have to say, to ask: 'Why do these terrible things happen?' instead of simply reacting."[136]

Resources

CRITICAL RESISTANCE: BEYOND THE
PRISON-INDUSTRIAL COMPLEX
www.criticalresistance.org
National Office:
1904 Franklin Street, Suite 504
Oakland, CA 94612
Phone: (510) 444-0484
Fax: (510) 444-2177
crnational@criticalresistance.org

NORTHEAST REGIONAL OFFICE
460 W. 128th Street
New York, NY 10027
Phone: (917) 493-9795
Fax: (917) 493-9798
crne@criticalresistance.org

SOUTHERN REGIONAL OFFICE
P.O. Box 791213
New Orleans, LA 70179
Phone: (504) 837-5348 or toll free (866) 579-0885
crsouth@criticalresistance.org

HUMAN RIGHTS WATCH PRISON PROJECT
350 5th Avenue, 34th Floor
New York, NY 10118-3299
Phone: (212) 290-4700
Fax: (212) 736-1300
hrwnyc@hrw.org
www.hrw.org

INCITE! WOMEN OF COLOR AGAINST VIOLENCE
P.O. Box 6861
Minneapolis, MN 55406-0861
Phone: (415) 553-3837
incite-national@yahoo.com
www.incite-national.org/

JUSTICE NOW (JUSTICE NETWORK ON WOMEN)
1322 Webster Street, Suite 210
Oakland, CA 94612
Phone: (510) 839-7654
Fax: (510) 839-7615
cynthia@jnow.org, cassandra@jnow.org
www.jnow.org

THE NATIONAL CENTER ON INSTITUTIONS
AND ALTERNATIVES (NCIA)
3125 Mt. Vernon Avenue
Alexandria, VA 22305
Phone: (703) 684-0373
Fax: (703) 549-4077
info@ncianet.org
www.ncianet.org/ncia; www.sentencing.org

PRISON ACTIVIST RESOURCE CENTER
P.O. Box 339
Berkeley, CA 94701
Phone: (510) 893-4648
Fax: (510) 893-4607
parc@prisonactivist.org
www.prisonactivist.org

PRISON LEGAL NEWS
2400 NW 80th Street, PMB #148
Seattle, WA 98117
Phone: (206) 781-6524
www.prisonlegalnews.org

PRISON MORATORIUM PROJECT
388 Atlantic Avenue, 3rd Floor
Brooklyn, NY 11217
Phone: (718) 260-8805
Fax: (212) 727-8616
pmp@nomoreprisons.org
www.nomoreprisons.org

THE SENTENCING PROJECT
514-10th Street NW #1000
Washington, DC 20004
Phone: (202) 628-0871
Fax: (202) 628-1091
www.sentencingproject.org

Notes

1   Katherine Stapp, "Prisons Double as Mental Wards," *Asheville Global Report*, no. 164 (7–13 March 2002), www.agrnews.org. Stapp's article describes a study by Seena Fazel of Oxford University and John Danesh of Cambridge University published in the British medical journal *The Lancet*. According to Stapp, the researchers concluded, "One in seven inmates suffers from a mental illness that could be a risk factor for suicide, says the study. This represents more than one million people in Western countries. The study's authors . . . surveyed data on the mental health of 23,000 prisoners in 12 Western countries over a period of three decades. They found that prisoners 'were several times more likely to have psychosis and major depression, and about 10 times more likely to have anti-social personality disorder, than the general population.'"

2   Elliot Currie, *Crime and Punishment in America* (New York: Henry Holt and Company, 1998), 21.

3   Mike Davis, "Hell Factories in the Field: A Prison-Industrial Complex," *The Nation* 260, no.7 (20 February 1995).

4   The information in this paragraph regarding the dates California prisons opened was taken from the Web site of the California Department of Corrections. www.cdc.state.ca.us/facility/facil.htm.

5   www.cdc.state.ca.us/facility/instvspw.htm.

6   www.cdc.state.ca.us/facility/factsht.htm.

7   www.cdc.state.ca.us/facility/instccwf.htm.

8   Sandow Birk, *Incarcerated: Visions of California in the Twenty-First Century* (San Francisco: Last Gasp of San Francisco, 2001).

9   Ruth Wilson Gilmore, "Globalisation and U.S. Prison Growth: From Military Keynesianism to Post-Keynesian Militarism," *Race and Class* 40 no. 2/3 (October 1998–March 1999): 174.

10   Gilmore, 184.

11   Gina Dent, "Stranger Inside and Out: Black Subjectivity in the Women-in-Prison Film," in *Black Cultural Traffic: Crossroads in Black Performance and Black Popular Culture*, edited by Harry Elam and Kennel Jackson (Ann Arbor: University of Michigan Press, forthcoming 2003).

12   Marc Mauer, "Young Men and the Criminal Justice System: A Growing National Problem" (Washington, D.C.: The Sentencing Project, 1990).

13   Marc Mauer and Tracy Huling, "Young Black Americans and the Criminal Justice System: Five Years Later" (Washington, D.C.: The Sentencing Project, 1995).

14   Allen J. Beck, Jennifer C. Karberg, and Paige M. Harrison, "Prison and Jail Inmates at Midyear 2001," Bureau of Justice Statistics Bulletin (Washington, D.C.: U.S. Department of Justice, Office of Justice Programs, April 2002, NCJ 191702), 12.

15   Adam Jay Hirsh, *The Rise of the Penitentiary: Prisons and Punishment in Early America* (New Haven and London: Yale University Press, 1992), 84.

16   Ibid., 71.

17   Ibid., 73.

18   Ibid., 74–75.

19   Milton Fierce, *Slavery Revisited: Blacks and the Southern Convict Lease System, 1865–1933* (New York: African Studies Research Center, Brooklyn College, City University of New York, 1994), 85–86.

20   Mary Ann Curtin, *Black Prisoners and Their World, Alabama, 1865–1900* (Charlottesville and London: University Press of Virginia, 2000), 6.

21   Curtin, 42.

22   Phillip S. Foner, ed. *The Life and Writings of Frederick Douglass. Volume 4: Reconstruction and After* (New York: International Publishers, 1955), 379.

23   Cheryl Harris, "Whiteness as Property," in *Critical Race Theory*, by Kimberlé Crenshaw, Neil Gotanda, Gary Peller, and Kendall Thomas. (New York: The New Press, 1995).

24   On March 1, 2003, the INS was officially disestablished and its operations were folded into the new Department of Homeland Security.

25 Matthew J. Mancini, *One Dies, Get Another: Convict Leasing in the American South, 1866–1928* (Columbia, S.C.: South Carolina Press, 1996), 25.

26 Ibid.

27 David Oshinsky, *"Worse Than Slavery": Parchman Farm and the Ordeal of Jim Crow Justice* (New York: The Free Press, 1996).

28 Alex Lichtenstein, *Twice the Work of Free Labor: The Political Economy of Convict Labor in the New South* (London, New York: Verso), 1996.

29 Oshinsky, 45.

30 Curtin, 44.

31 Lichtenstein, 13.

32 Ibid., xix.

33 Ibid.

34 Curtin, 1.

35 Curtin, 213–14.

36 Michel Foucault, *Discipline and Punish: The Birth of the Prison* (New York: Vintage Books, 1979), 234.

37 Ibid., 3.

38 Louis J. Palmer Jr., *The Death Penalty: An American Citizen's Guide to Understanding Federal and State Laws* (Jefferson, N.C., and London: McFarland & Co, Inc. Publishers, 1998).

39 Russell P. Dobash, R. Emerson Dobash, and Sue Gutteridge, *The Imprisonment of Women* (Oxford: Basil Blackwell, 1986), 19.

40 John Hirst, "The Australian Experience: The Convict Colony," In *The Oxford History of the Prison: The Practice of Punishment in Western Society,* edited by Norval Morris and David J. Rothman (New York, Oxford: Oxford University Press, 1998), 244.

41 Cesare Beccaria, *On Crimes and Punishments* (Cambridge: Cambridge University Press, 1995).

42 See Georg Rusche and Otto Kirchheimer, *Punishment and Social Structure* (New York: Columbia University Press, 1939), and Dario Melossi and Massimo Pavarini, *The Prison and the Factory: Origins of the Penitentiary System* (Totowa, N.J: Barnes and Noble Books, 1981).

43 Estelle B. Freedman, *Their Sisters' Keepers: Women's Prison Reform in America, 1830–1930* (Ann Arbor: University of Michigan Press, 1984), 10.

44 See discussion of John Howard's 1777 report, *The State of the Prisons in England and Wales*, in *A Just Measure of Pain: The Penitentiary in the Industrial Revolution, 1750–1850*, by Michael Ignatieff (New York: Pantheon Books, 1978).

45 Jeremy Bentham, *The Panopticon and Other Prison Writings* (London and New York: Verso, 1995).

46 Charles Dickens, *The Works of Charles Dickens, Vol. 27, American Notes* (New York: Peter Fenelon Collier and Son, 1900), 119–20.

47 Gustave de Beaumont and Alexis de Tocqueville, *On the Penitentiary System in the United States and its Application in France* (Carbondale and Edwardsville: Southern Illinois University Press), 1964 [1833].

48 Beaumont and Tocqueville, 131.

49 "Cold Storage: Super-Maximum Security Confinement in Indiana," A Human Rights Watch Report (New York: Human Rights Watch, October 1997), 13.

50 "Cold Storage," 18–19.

51 For an extended discussion of the Supermax, see Craig Haney and Mona Lynch, "Regulating Prisons of the Future: A Psychological Analysis of Supermax and Solitary Confinement," *New York University Review of Law and Social Change* 23 (1997): 477–570.

52 "Cold Storage," 19.

53 Chase Riveland, "Supermax Prisons: Overview and General Considerations." (Washington, D.C.: National Institute of Corrections, U.S. Department of Justice, January 1999), 4.

54 John Bender, *Imagining the Penitentiary: Fiction and the Architecture of Mind in Eighteenth-Century England* (Chicago and London: University of Chicago Press, 1987), 2.

55 Ignatieff, 47.

56 Ibid., 53.

57 Bender, 1.

58 Ignatieff, 58.

59 Ibid., 52.

60 Bender, 29.

61 Ibid., 31.

62 Robert Burns, *I Am a Fugitive from a Georgia Chaingang* (Savannah, Ga.: Beehive Press, 1994).

63   George Jackson, *Soledad Brother: The Prison Letters of George Jackson* (Westport, Conn.: Lawrence Hill and Co., 1994).

64   Bettina Aptheker and Angela Davis, eds. *If They Come in the Morning: Voices of Resistance* (New York: Third Press, 1971).

65   Mumia Abu-Jamal, *Live from Death Row* (New York: Addison-Wesley Publishing Company, 1995), 65–67.

66   Mumia Abu-Jamal, *Death Blossoms* (Farmington, Pa.: The Plough Publishing House, 1997).

67   Mumia Abu-Jamal, *All Things Censored* (New York: Seven Stories Press, 2000).

68   Section 20411 of the Violent Crime Control and Law Enforcement Act of 1994 prohibited the award of Pell Grants to fund prisoners' education. It remains in effect today. See usinfo.state.gov/infousa/laws/majorlaws/h3355_en.htm.

69   H. Bruce Franklin, ed. *Prison Writing in Twentieth-Century America* (New York: Penguin Books, 1998), 13.

70   Malcolm X, *The Autobiography of Malcolm X (As Told to Alex Haley)* (New York: Random House, 1965).

71   *The Last Graduation*, directed by Barbara Zahm. (Zahm Productions and Deep Dish TV, 1997).

72   Marcia Bunney, "One Life in Prison: Perception, Reflection, and Empowerment," in *Harsh Punishment: International Experiences of Women's Imprisonment*, edited by Sandy Cook and Susanne Davies (Boston: Northeastern University Press, 1999), 29–30.

73   Assata Shakur, *Assata: An Autobiography* (Westport, Conn.: Lawrence Hill and Co., 1987).

74   Ibid., x.

75   Ibid., 83–84.

76   Elizabeth Gurley Flynn, *The Alderson Story: My Life as a Political Prisoner* (New York: International Publishers, 1972).

77   ACE (Members of AIDS Counseling and Education), *Breaking the Walls of Silence: AIDS and Women in a New York State Maximum Security Prison* (New York: Overlook Press, 1998).

78   Vivien Stern, *A Sin Against the Future: Imprisonment in the World* (Boston: Northeastern Press, 1998), 138.

79   See Elaine Showalter, "Victorian Women and Insanity," in *Madhouses, Mad-Doctors and Madmen: The Social History of Psychiatry in the*

Victorian Era, edited by Andrew Scull (Philadelphia: University of Pennsylvania Press), 1981.

80   Luana Ross, *Inventing the Savage: The Social Construction of Native American Criminality.* (Austin: University of Texas Press, 1998), 121.

81   Freedman, 15.

82   See Freedman, chapters 3 and 4.

83   Joanne Belknap, *The Invisible Woman: Gender, Crime, and Justice* (Belmont, Calif.: Watsworth Publishing Company), 95.

84   Lucia Zedner, "Wayward Sisters: The Prison for Women," in *The Oxford History of the Prison: The Practice of Punishment in Western Society,* edited by Norval Morris and David J. Rothman (New York: Oxford University Press), 318.

85   Ibid., 318.

86   Currie, 14.

87   Ross, 89.

88   Ibid., 90.

89   Tekla Dennison Miller, *The Warden Wore Pink* (Brunswick, Me.: Biddle Publishing Company, 1996), 97–98.

90   Ibid., 100.

91   Ibid., 121.

92   *Philadelphia Daily News*, 26 April 1996.

93   American Civil Liberties Union Freedom Network, 26 August 1996, aclu.org/news/w82696b.html.

94   *All Too Familiar: Sexual Abuse of Women in U.S. State Prisons* (New York: Human Rights Watch, December 1996), 1.

95   Ibid., 2.

96   www.oneword.org/ips2/aug98/03_56_003.

97   *Standard Minimum Rules for the Treatment of Prisoners* (adopted by the First United Nations Congress on the Prevention of Crime and the Treatment of Offenders, held at Geneva in 1955, and approved by the Economic and Social Council by its resolution 663 C (XXIV) of 31 July 1957 and 2076 (LXII) of 13 May 1977).

98   Amanda George, "Strip Searches: Sexual Assault by the State," www.aic.gov.au/publications/proceedings/20/george.pdf, 211–12.

99   Amanda George made this comment in the video *Strip Search*. Produced by Simmering Video and Coalition Against Police Violence (date unavailable).

100 Linda Evans and Eve Goldberg, "The Prison Industrial Complex and the Global Economy" (pamphlet) (Berkeley. Calif.: Prison Activist Resource Center, 1997).

101 See note 3.

102 *Wall Street Journal*, 12 May 1994.

103 Ibid.

104 Allen M. Hornblum, *Acres of Skin: Human Experiments at Holmesburg Prison* (New York: Routledge, 1998), xvi.

105 Hornblum, 212.

106 Hornblum, 37.

107 See A.S. Relman, "The New Medical Industrial Complex," *New England Journal of Medicine* 30 (17) (23 October 1980): 963–70.

108 Vince Beiser, "How We Got to Two Million: How Did the Land of the Free Become the World's Leading Jailer?" *Debt to Society*, MotherJones.com Special Report, 10 July 2001. Available at: www.motherjones.com/prisons/overview.html, 6.

109 Paige M. Harrison and Allen J. Beck, "Prisoners in 2001," Bureau of Justice Statistics Bulletin (Washington, D.C.: U.S. Department of Justice, Office of Justice Programs, July 2002, NCJ 195189), 1.

110 Allen Beck and Paige M. Harrison., "Prisoners in 2000," Bureau of Justice Statistics Bulletin (Washington, D.C.: U.S. Department of Justice, Office of Justice Programs, August 2001, NCJ 1888207), 1.

111 Harrison and Beck, "Prisoners in 2001."

112 Steve Donziger, *The Real War on Crime: Report of the National Criminal Justice Commission* (New York: Perennial Publishers, 1996), 87.

113 Allen J. Beck, Jennifer C. Karberg, and Paige M. Harrison. "Prison and Jail Inmates at Midyear 2001," Bureau of Justice Statistics Bulletin (Washington, D.C., U.S. Department of Justice, Office of Justice Programs, April 2002, NCJ 191702), 12.

114 Harrison and Beck, "Prisoners in 2001," 7.

115 Ibid.

116 Sue Anne Pressley, "Texas County Sued by Missouri Over Alleged Abuse of Inmates," *Washington Post*, 27 August 1997, A2.

117 Madeline Baro, "Video Prompts Prison Probe," *Philadelphia Daily News,* 20 August 1997.

118 "Beatings Worse Than Shown on Videotape, Missouri Inmates Say." The Associated Press, 27 August 1997, 7:40 P.M. EDT.

119 Joel Dyer, *The Perpetual Prison Machine: How America Profits from Crime* (Boulder, Col.: Westview Press, 2000).

120 Abby Ellin, "A Food Fight Over Private Prisons," *New York Times,* Education Life, Sunday, 8 April 2001.

121 See Julia Sudbury, "Mules and Other Hybrids: Incarcerated Women and the Limits of Diaspora," *Harvard Journal of African American Public Policy,* Fall 2002.

122 Amanda George, "The New Prison Culture: Making Millions from Misery," in Sandy Cook and Susanne Davies, *Harsh Punishment: International Experiences of Women's Imprisonment,* by Sandy Cook and Susanne Davies (Boston: Northeastern Press, 1999), 190.

123 Press release issued by Wackenhut, 23 August 2002.

124 Ibid.

125 Dyer, 14.

126 See Amnesty International Press Release at www.geocities.com/turkish-hungerstrike/amapril.html.

127 www.hrw.org/wr2k2/prisons.html

128 www.suntimes.co.za/20

129 Arthur Waskow, resident, Institute for Policy Studies, *Saturday Review,* 8 January 1972, quoted in Fay Honey Knopp, et al., *Instead of Prisons: A Handbook for Abolitionists* (Syracuse, N.Y.: Prison Research Education Action Project, 1976), 15–16.

130 www.bettyfordcenter.org/programs/programs/index.html

131 www.bettyfordcenter.org/programs/programs/prices.html

132 Herman Bianchi, "Abolition: Assensus and Sanctuary," in *Abolitionism: Toward a Non-Repressive Approach to Crime,* eds. Herman Bianchi and René Swaaningen (Amsterdam: Free University Press, 1986), 117.

133 Anthropologist Nancy Schepper-Hughes described this astonishing turn of events in a talk she delivered at UC Berkeley on September 24, 2001, entitled "Un-Doing: The Politics of the Impossible in the New South Africa."

134 Bella English, "Why Do They Forgive Us," *Boston Globe,* 23 April 2003.

135   Ibid.

136   Gavin Du Venage, "Our Daughter's Killers Are Now Our Friends," *The Straits Times* (Singapore), 2 December 2 2001.

About the Author

ANGELA YVONNE DAVIS is a professor of history of consciousness at the University of California, Santa Cruz. Over the last thirty years, she has been active in numerous organizations challenging prison-related repression. Her advocacy on behalf of political prisoners led to three capital charges, sixteen months in jail awaiting trial, and a highly publicized campaign then acquittal in 1972. In 1973, the National Committee to Free Angela Davis and All Political Prisoners, along with the Attica Brothers, the American Indian Movement and other organizations founded the National Alliance Against Racist and Political Repression, of which she remained co-chairperson for many years. In 1998, she was one of the twenty-five organizers of the historic Berkeley conference "Critical Resistance: Beyond the Prison Industrial Complex" and since that time has served as convener of a research group bearing the same name under the auspices of the University of California Humanities Research Institute. Angela is author of many books, including *Blues Legacies and Black Feminism: Gertrude "Ma" Rainey, Bessie Smith, and Billie Holiday*. Her new book, forthcoming from Random House, is *Prisons and Democracy*.

Bill Barnes

ARE PRISONS OBSOLETE?